THE SECOND BOUNCE OF THE BALL

THE SECOND BOUNCE OF THE BALL

Turning risk into opportunity

Ronald Cohen
with Terry Ilott

Weidenfeld & Nicolson
LONDON

First published in Great Britain in 2007
by Weidenfeld & Nicolson

3 5 7 9 10 8 6 4

Text © Ronald Cohen 2007
Cartoons © Bill Whitehead 2007

A CIP catalogue record for this book
is available from the British Library.

ISBN: 978 0 297 85147 9
ISBN: 978 0 297 85148 6

Typeset by Input Data Services Ltd, Frome

Printed in Great Britain by Mackays of Chatham plc, Chatham, Kent

Weidenfeld & Nicolson

The Orion Publishing Group Ltd
Orion House
5 Upper Saint Martin's Lane
London, WC2H 9EA

An Hachette Livre UK Company

www.orionbooks.co.uk

To my parents, Michael and Sonia, to Sharon,
my wife, and to our children Tamara and Jonathan,
who have been my closest partners in everything.

Acknowledgements

It was Lord Weidenfeld who encouraged me in my intention, when I stepped down from the chairmanship of Apax, to distil my experience into a book. I spent some time working on the basic concepts and structure, and, having an idea of what I wanted to say, I turned to former journalist, author and sometime entrepreneur, Terry Ilott, to help me say it. Terry and I spent a year working on the text together.

André and Sonia Cohen, Peter Englander, Edward Gera, Michele Giddens, David Gillerman, Tom Hampson-Bellon, Yossi, Julie, David and Ron Harel, Sharon, Tamara and Johnny Harel-Cohen, Alisa Helbitz, Sir Christopher Hogg, Richard Holmes, Tal Keinan, Rebecca Kemsley, Dr Avigdor Klagsbald, Siobhan Loftus, Alan Patricof, Andrew and Simon de Picot, Jill Potter, Sir Harry Solomon, Dr Miriam Stoppard, Maurice Tchénio and Dr Heather Wood read drafts and provided incisive criticism. Sir Martin Gilbert not only gave general editorial comments but made detailed corrections and suggestions on style and compiled the index. Noemi Rav came up with helpful design solutions. Bill Whitehead kindly gave me permission to reproduce cartoons that he had originally created for Apax Christmas cards. My agent, Mort Janklow, and the book's editor and publisher at Weidenfeld & Nicolson, Alan Samson, have guided the book into the marketplace with enthusiasm and expertise.

I also owe a debt of gratitude to my partners and colleagues at Apax who contributed so much to the success of our firm. Many of the insights in this book are based on our shared ideas and experiences.

All the above contributed greatly to this book and to all of them I am grateful. Responsibility for the content of the book and its shortcomings is, of course, mine alone.

Contents

INTRODUCTION

Exploiting uncertainty is the essence of entrepreneurship.

This is a book about what it takes to become a successful entrepreneur. It is written for entrepreneurs and for those who are interested in entrepreneurship, whatever their age, wherever they are, whether they have already set out on the entrepreneurial road or are contemplating doing so.

Entrepreneurship is a way of thinking that can be applied to all avenues in life. It is a way of looking at the world, a mindset that is sharpened and improved by experience.

I have encountered every kind of obstacle, as well as every kind of opportunity, in my career as an entrepreneur, building a major firm whose business has been investing in other entrepreneurial businesses. As an investor, I have mostly backed winners. Inevitably, I have also backed some losers. I have been successful in part because

I have thought long and hard about enterprise every day of my working life, and I have learned from my mistakes.

I have distilled what I have learned into this book.

My purpose is, first, to make readers aware of the road they will travel and the challenges they will face in their entrepreneurial careers; and, second, to provide some pointers about how best to achieve success.

The fundamental insight that I would take from my experience in building Apax Partners, and from my observation of the hundreds of companies in which Apax has made investments, is that entrepreneurs, if they are to be successful, must seek out and take advantage of situations of uncertainty.

If you want to build a thriving business you have to see beyond today's certainties to tomorrow's uncertainties. You have to look at what is going to happen next in your field and put yourself in a position to take advantage of it.

It is like a bouncing ball. If you were looking today for a pharmaceutical opportunity, you might guess that the current bounce is the obesity market: that is where the drug companies are directing much of their research. But the smart pharmaceutical entrepreneur is already thinking beyond that – to the next bounce of the obesity ball. The next bounce could be the opportunity on which to build a thriving business.

In my own field, private equity, the first bounce was private placements of venture capital for start-up investments. The second bounce was the raising of discretionary early-stage, venture-capital funds. The next bounce was buy-out funds focused on more mature businesses. Subsequent bounces included the moves towards sector specialization, regional funds and global funds. At every stage, I had to keep my eye on the next bounce of the ball, so that I could take advantage of it. If I did not, those of my competitors who did would leave me behind.

Returning to the example of obesity: obese people are extremely unfit. Having been obese for years, they have not had the opportunity to exercise. So the next bounce of that ball might be to enable post-obese people to become fit, by specializing in the particular muscular and cosmetic problems from which obese people suffer. But how valid is that observation? And, if it is valid, how do you take advantage of it? What product or service is likely to prove popular and profit-able? How can you be sure that the product you deliver will be competitive with the other products that are aimed at the same market opportunity?

These questions are all an expression of the same thing: uncertainty. Uncertainty and opportunity go together.

Fortunately, the future has its origins in the present. That is why I use the analogy of the bouncing ball. We can all see where the ball is bouncing today; we know it has to bounce somewhere tomorrow. But few of us try to anticipate where tomorrow's bounce will be, and even fewer will attempt to take advantage of it.

The uncertainty about exactly where and when the ball will bounce provides the opportunity for the entrepreneur. It is a rule that you cannot make fortunes out of situations of certainty; market forces make sure that the returns are low if everybody can take equal advantage of the same opportunity. The risks involved in government bonds are minimal. They pay a predictable and low rate of interest. Everyone has equal access. Consequently, you cannot make a high return by holding government bonds. It is only in situations of uncertainty that opportunity for significant gain arises.

As I will explain later in this book, by looking closely at the ball and its trajectory you can reduce the element of uncertainty: what seems to other people to be very uncertain seems to the informed entrepreneur much less uncertain.

There is a cliché that entrepreneurs are born, not made. If I think back on my experience, I know this is not entirely true. Yes, all entrepreneurs share certain personality traits: a high level of confidence and high levels of optimism, energy and determination. But the people who become entrepreneurs come in all ages, shapes and sizes, and their entrepreneurial skills vary considerably.

There has been a significant increase in the number of entrepreneurs during the three decades in which I have been a professional investor. This speaks not so much for a sudden growth in the gene pool of 'born' entrepreneurs, as for the opportunities that have opened up for all kinds of people to use their entrepreneurial ability. Major waves of entrepreneurship have been forming in the world for the past thirty years, first in the United States, then across Europe and Israel, and now across Asia.

Not only are there more entrepreneurs than ever, but a significant proportion of the workforce is employed by firms backed by the principal entrepreneurial investors: the venture-capital and private-equity funds. Many more people today are touched by enterprise than was the case when I started out in the early 1970s. This book is, I hope, a timely contribution to the understanding of entrepreneurship, including the roles of venture capital and private equity, as well as a guide to becoming a successful entrepreneur.

Many potential entrepreneurs who could start out have not started out. Many have failed who could have been successful. The reason is that they are not equipped. They have not grasped the fundamentals. Because few entrepreneurs have an overall view of what is involved

4

in creating a successful venture, they have to learn about entre-preneurship the hard way: from their mistakes. Such learning is at the cost of considerable time and hardship. This book is not a total substitute for experience – no book could hope to be that – but it should help you save time and hardship, and, hopefully, avoid some costly mistakes.

Today's entrepreneur does not have to be like a nineteenth-century explorer, heading off into the unknown without a map. This book is a map, drawn from more than thirty years' experience.

If I have been successful in distilling what I have learned, this book could help a generation who feel that they would like to do something entrepreneurial with their careers, but wonder whether they can really be successful. They ask: 'Is it realistic for me to aspire to building a successful business?'

This book sets out the road to be travelled; it describes the qualities and skills of those who have travelled it successfully before you; and it discusses the principles that ensure you reach your destination.

It is the book that would have been useful to me when I started out in 1972. It would have been useful to have confirmation that launching out at the age of twenty-six was not too young; that I was right to start with the idea that I was building a large business, and to channel my energies into putting in place the infrastructure needed to become a market leader; and that, given my diligence, my likely ability to attract good people to work with me and my aptitude for the sector I had picked, if I just stuck with it I would be successful.

Start young, think big, stick with it: that is valuable advice that I did not get, but which I can now offer the aspiring entrepreneur.

Some people think that if you want to be an entrepreneur the

5

Start young,
think big,
stick with it

important thing is to be bold and get started. Being bold is important, but it is not enough. A good entrepreneur does not start out blindfold, thinking, 'I'm just going to go wherever my feet lead me.' What good entrepreneurs have in common is clear vision – as well as a capacity for taking infinite pains to achieve that vision.

Good entrepreneurs realize that the foundations you lay down limit the size of the edifice you will build. If you build in a modular way, you can add as you go along. If you start by pitching a tent on the site, you cannot build on it at all.

In my own industry, private equity, the winners over the last thirty years have been those who combined the clearest and most ambitious vision with the skills needed to achieve it.

Building a successful business is not easy. It will consume years, it will demand attention to detail and it will test your nerves, stamina and capacity for hard work to the limit. As I make clear in the book, entrepreneurship is not for the faint-hearted. But it will be easier if you know what to expect and how to go about dealing with it. This book seeks to inform you on both counts.

In the first chapter I describe who I am and how I got started; I provide relevant background on the development of modern-day entrepreneurship and of the principal source of entrepreneurial finance, the venture-capital and private-equity industry; and I discuss the role that stock exchanges play in the development of early-stage businesses. All this is seen through the prism of my experience at Apax. I then ask the reader to consider who he or she might be: my purpose is to establish whether entrepreneurship is really for you.

I look at the elements that make opportunities more or less attract-ive, before explaining what I mean by the second bounce of the ball and why anticipating where and when it will bounce is so important for success.

The first four chapters of the book are all about aptitude and the right opportunity. They are followed by the conclusions I have drawn regarding the key resources required to take advantage of opportunity: the right people and the right money. I then discuss the personal qualities required to manage an entrepreneurial business, and the roles played by personality and luck.

In chapter nine, I underline the importance of ethics.

I conclude by addressing the challenge of succession, and what life might have in store for the entrepreneurial leader once the company has been floated or sold, or when the mantle of leadership has passed to a new generation.

If you are thinking of an entrepreneurial career, this book will have served its purpose if it helps you to define your attitude towards uncertainty and your ability to exploit it; to assess properly the opportunities before you; to judge timing in relation to business cycles and market trends; to adapt your role as leader to the needs of your business and to attract the best people to your team; to take into account the financial dimension of your proposed venture; to turn setbacks to your advantage; to make the right decisions quickly and effectively; and to understand that high ethical standards are not only desirable but essential.

This is not a how-to book, in the sense of providing a plan, a checklist, exercises and tips. The subject is too complex for that. Nor is the advice given on the following pages about the details of implementation. It is certainly not part of my purpose to tell anyone how to write a business plan. Rather, the book shows you how to approach an entrepreneurial opportunity and how to put yourself in a position to best take advantage of it. In so far as I lay down any rules at all, they are higher-level rules, the fundamentals of entrepreneurial strategy.

If I have achieved my objective, the book will help you decide if an entrepreneurial career is for you, and show you how to make a real success of it.

1

CLIMBING THE NORTH FACE

The higher you aim, the higher you go.

When do you discover that you are cut out to be an entrepreneur? To answer this question, it might be useful to look at the example of my own career. I was born in Cairo. As a child I spoke French at home; Arabic was my second language; I did not speak English at all. Then, when I was eleven years old, President Nasser's reaction to the Suez crisis made the life of a Jewish family like ours very difficult. Because my mother carried a British passport, we were forced to leave. We were allowed to take ten Egyptian pounds and a suitcase each; we had to leave everything else behind. I left clutching my stamp collection and I remember worrying that somebody might take it away from me. We moved to London.

Once we were settled in, I went to a state school in north-west London. I started with the disadvantage of not speaking the language. Even so, I performed reasonably well in my first year, especially in those subjects where mastery of English was not required. By my second year, I had grasped the language sufficiently to move up to the top of the class. I was aided by an outstanding teacher of history, Richard Farley, who had a brilliant mind and a breadth of knowledge the like of which I have not encountered since. It was he who prepared me for the Oxford University entrance exams. He gave me a list of more than 200 books to read. In the space of a year, I read them all and discussed each one with him. As the years have passed, I have come to realize just how much I owe him: he taught me to question conventional wisdom, to think for myself and to have confidence in my own opinions. I tracked him down a couple of years ago: at the age of eighty-four, he was reading as widely as ever.

I studied Politics, Philosophy and Economics (PPE) at Oxford. Again, I was both an active and an ambitious student and in my third year opted for what might be called public life by standing for – and winning – the presidency of the Oxford Union, the leading debating society in the English-speaking world. The high point of my presidency was Robert Kennedy's acceptance of an invitation to speak. There were crowds when he arrived; he stood on the roof of a car to speak to them in the street before going in to address the students in the debating hall.

At Oxford, I did not really think about the road beyond. My father, Michael, forced to start all over again in Britain, did quite well in business at first, but my parents' financial future was not assured. Providing them with some measure of security was an obligation of which I was very aware. By the time I left Oxford in 1967, my father was fifty-four years old. At the age of thirty he had moved from working for a bank into setting up his own trading business, importing and exporting goods to and from Egypt. Perhaps it was from him that I picked up the idea of working for myself.

I was very much a product of the 1960s: idealistic and wanting to make a difference. But I would have to make money somehow. My father suggested that I would be better prepared for employment if I completed my education by going to Harvard Business School (HBS). It appealed to me: I knew that when I came out of Harvard I would have skills that would be helpful to me whatever my career.

I contacted HBS, asking if I could apply and what scholarships might be available. The Henry Fellowship, which each year provided for two American students to come to Britain and two British students to go to the United States, was still open. I had to go before a panel of judges comprising some of the intellectual luminaries of Oxford at the time, Isaiah Berlin among them.

The rules of the Henry Fellowship meant that I could go to either Harvard or Yale to read the subject of my choice. I hesitated briefly between Harvard Business School and Yale Law School, but followed my first instinct: I thought I would probably benefit more from business school than law school, and, anyway, I did not see myself as a lawyer. My intuition told me that being in a service role would not suit me. My ambition was not yet fully formed, but I knew that I was attracted to a leadership role of some kind.

The Henry Fellowship paid for only the first year of studies. I had to make my own arrangements for the second. I turned to the student franchises that were available on campus to help pay for my second year.

One franchise was to prepare the Prospectus: a publication with photographs and biographical details of every student coming into the new class. It was a much-used reference book and therefore attracted a certain amount of advertising. I teamed up with a fellow student by the name of Al Fullerton to bid for this franchise. Al prepared the publication and I went to New York to sell advertising space. In three days I sold more than enough advertising for our needs. This first attempt at entrepreneurship provided part of the money for my fees.

Another part of my income came when I heard that if I bought a British car, I could sell it at the end of the year at a profit, as well as enjoying the use of it in the meantime. I took a bank loan and bought a white Triumph convertible. As predicted, I later sold it at a profit.

At my London school there had been, academically speaking, a number of promising racehorses. At Oxford there was a larger number of racehorses. At Harvard it was all racehorses. What Oxford had taught me was the importance of underlying principles. What Harvard taught me was the additional importance of studying the small print, of reading the footnotes. HBS students were hugely motivated, competitive and ambitious, and they focused on every detail.

It was at Harvard that I made my first real contact with the world of business and money.

In those days ambitious business-school graduates looked forward to careers in big business, not enterprise. But, as luck would have it, I arrived – in 1967 – just in time to witness the beginning of two waves that, over the next three decades, were to change the shape of business around the world. The first was the wave of entrepreneurship in new, hi-tech industries such as information technology and life sciences. The second was the wave of venture capital that financed the hi-tech entrepreneurs.

If I were to pinpoint a date at which these two waves first came to public attention, it would probably be in 1968, the year that saw both the launch of Intel, now the world's largest semi-conductor company, and the stock-market flotation of Digital Equipment Corporation (DEC). Both firms were connected to the emerging computer industry, both were American and both were founded by technically accomplished and now legendary entrepreneurs: Intel by Robert Noyce and Gordon Moore, and DEC by Ken Olsen.

The first modern venture capitalist was probably General Georges Doriot, who was a visiting lecturer at HBS when I was there. He had been responsible for an investment of $70,000 to help launch DEC back in 1959. DEC floated in 1968 at a valuation of $125 million. Doriot's firm, American Research and Development (ARD), made an annualized return on its investment in excess of 100 per cent: it doubled its money each year.

The entrepreneurial wave was starting to form, but those who noticed it were in the minority. Attention was still focused on the established corporate giants. These were the years of *The American Challenge*, the best-selling book by French government minister Jean-Jacques Servan-Schreiber, who predicted that American corporations were likely to dominate Europe and the world over the coming years.

To me, it seemed that Servan-Schreiber would be proved wrong. Europe was still rebuilding after the devastation of the Second World War and only needed time to reassert itself. Sure, big American companies would buy big companies in Europe, but soon enough big companies in Europe would start buying big companies in America.

It was to become clear, however, that many of these large corporations – American and European – were not as robust as they appeared. As the economy became more global and as old products and markets found themselves overtaken by new technology, so some large, established firms were to lose ground and shed jobs. It would be up to a new generation of entrepreneurs to create jobs in their place.

It was among innovative companies such as DEC that the United States turned out to have crucial advantages over Europe. One advantage was in education, especially in the area of new technology. A second was in the business culture, which admired success in business, welcomed innovation and encouraged competition and risk-taking. A third was in easy access to capital. Start-ups and early-stage companies in America were soon to find backers in the growing community of venture-capital investors, and among institutional as well as individual investors in the shares traded on the Nasdaq stock market, which was created in 1970.

Hence, a real opportunity for me and my contemporaries was going to be in entrepreneurship rather than in big business. I was never going to be a hi-tech entrepreneur, given my low-tech background, but the idea of setting up an investment company to support entrepreneurs matched my skills and appealed to me greatly. This would be my opportunity to achieve entrepreneurial success.

Three of my fellow students felt the same. Two were French and one was an American whom I had first met at Oxford and who had turned up at Harvard Law School. We had dinners in a pizza restaurant near Harvard Square and talked about what we might do together. We knew we wanted to launch a venture. The appeal of doing something entrepreneurial was that, if we were successful, we would have the satisfaction of having created our own business from scratch. Building a business is like climbing a mountain. It presents a great challenge and, if you get to the top, there is a great sense of achievement. That desire for achievement was our motivation.

Our first entrepreneurial step was the creation, during my second year at Harvard, of a small mutual fund, the Redwood International Investors Fund, which we raised from personal acquaintances. Redwood made investments in small, American, publicly traded companies. Unfortunately, stock market performance proved weak and Redwood's returns were no better than average. After a couple of years, we returned the money with only a small profit. It was a valuable experience, nonetheless, and it made it more likely that our group would work together some time after graduation.

First, though, I had to get a job.

I felt I needed some business experience and I wanted to enhance my track record so that I would have something to fall back on should I need it.

As expected, Harvard made me eminently employable, and I got an offer from McKinsey, the management consultancy firm. I worked in the London office, in Jermyn Street, in a building once occupied by the great seventeenth-century scientist and mathematician, Sir Isaac Newton. Marvin Bower was the firm's leader at the time. I was looking forward to meeting him and one day I found myself coming out of the bathroom, where there happened to be no towels, with wet hands. Marvin Bower was coming towards me. He reached for my hand. There I was, straight out of college, and there he was, the already legendary guru of the consultancy world, engaging me in conversation while wiping his hand surreptitiously on his jacket.

I found consulting interesting, particularly because it taught me to understand a business quickly at a deep level, starting from scratch. But I soon realized that I would not be happiest as a consultant. My nature is not to advise but to do, and to lead.

I left McKinsey after about two years to reconnect with my

Harvard colleagues, some of whom had graduated after me, and to launch the company, Multinational Management Group (MMG), that was eventually to become Apax Partners.

Roger Morrison, a leading light at McKinsey in London, asked me why I was leaving. 'You could make partner here, you have a great future in the firm,' he told me. I replied that I wanted to do something more challenging. I said that I felt the view would be better if I travelled closer to the precipice. I had demonstrated ability and ambition at school, at Oxford, at Harvard and at McKinsey, and I felt that I could always go back to a consultancy job if necessary in the future, although I had no long-term desire to make a career as a consultant.

MMG had its origins in a Harvard Business School project written in 1970 by one of my partners, Maurice Tchénio. Maurice was a brilliant student – top of the class, a Baker Scholar – who graduated with high distinction. His paper was, in effect, a draft business plan for MMG, the name of which he had coined.

We launched MMG to provide advisory services to entre-preneurial companies. One of my colleagues was going to be based in his home town, Chicago, two were going back to Paris and I would be in London.

We got off to a good start when Maurice Tchénio suggested that we meet Maurice Schlogel, an outstanding personality and one of the top figures in European finance in the second half of the twentieth century. Schlogel had great faith in business school education and he offered to help us launch our business if we would help him with the launch of the state-financed French investment bank, the Institut de Dévelopement Industriel (IDI). He took us into the founding team of IDI and, eighteen months later, IDI put a small amount of money into MMG, 300,000 French francs (about $50,000). More importantly, Schlogel gave us the benefit of his reputation by becoming MMG's first chairman.

While we knew that we wanted to create a firm that was advising and, later, investing in growth businesses, young companies, by definition, were not able to pay significant advisory fees. Nor would the small companies in which we invested show meaningful returns for some years. In the meantime, we had to derive income from somewhere. So we focused on advising larger entrepreneurial companies on international expansion, raising capital through private placements, and advising on mergers and acquisitions (buying and selling companies or divisions of companies), especially where the transaction involved parties on both sides of the Atlantic.

It was, however, seemingly the worst time to start a venture like MMG, and successes were hard to achieve. The entrepreneurial wave that had started to form in the United States had not yet reached Europe, where there was no venture-capital or private-equity industry at all; rates of income tax were high (in Britain, the addition of a surcharge on investment income meant that the highest marginal rate of personal taxation was 98 per cent); and there was little entrepreneurial activity.

We tried to think out of the box. In the first year of our professional partnership, 1972, we considered what would have been one of the first private-equity buy-outs in Europe, of the French crane manufacturer Potain. For the deal to make financial sense, the equity investment had to be leveraged with a significant amount of debt (just as one mixes equity and debt when one raises a mortgage to buy a house). But in those days it proved impossible to raise the necessary debt for that kind of a transaction. We had the idea, but not the means. We were a decade too early.

To complicate matters further for me, 1973 saw three million unemployed in Britain, a global oil crisis and a British coal-miners' strike that led to a nationwide three-day working week; 1974 saw London's secondary banking crisis, in which several smaller banks went to the wall; and from 1974 to 1978 there was a deep recession.

Sure enough, we struggled, and in 1975 two of the founding partners, one in Chicago and one in Paris, pulled out. I attended a crisis meeting with Maurice Tchénio and our departing French partner at Maurice Schlogel's apartment on Avenue Foch in Paris.

Far-sighted as ever, Schlogel said to the departing partner, 'I think you are getting out at the wrong time. Venture capital is going to be big, it is the future.' His argument fell on deaf ears. I remember thinking as I came down in the elevator that this venture was not going to be as straightforward as I had first imagined.

After the departure of two members of our team, Maurice Tchénio made it clear that he, too, was jaundiced with the idea of the partnership. He was still prepared to work with me in France, but not as a close partner. He proposed that the partnership remain but that we each take responsibility for our own businesses. I was, in effect, on my own. I thought, 'Where do I go from here?'

I had a conversation with my father about what to do. I felt I could either take the high road, which was the more difficult option, and continue with MMG and rebuild almost from scratch, or I could reluctantly take the low road and get a job and then try to launch my own venture later. My father advised me to stick with it. I knew that developing an international firm advising and, more especially, investing in young, growth companies was the right thing to go for and, with my father's encouragement, I persevered. I had not turned my back on a career at McKinsey only to quit at the first obstacle.

I thought it was crucial formally to maintain the partnership even if two out of the original four were leaving and the two of us who remained were each going to be, in effect, largely autonomous. We had started three years earlier and I sensed the benefits of maintaining the firm's continuity. This is especially important in finance, a field where you need to be around for five or ten years before you begin to be trusted. I did not want to appear to have failed and started again.

With Maurice Schlogel's moral support, Maurice Tchénio and I stuck with it, albeit in more of an arm's length relationship than before. Neither of us was in for an easy journey. For the next nine years, every time I finished one corporate finance transaction I had to start another, just to earn the fees to cover my overheads. It was not until 1984 that I knew at the start of the year how I was going to cover my coming year's expenses, including my own salary. Only then, when I had two venture capital funds under management and the bulk of my revenues came from management fees rather than from corporate finance fees, did I have any level of financial security at all.

But by sticking with it, Maurice and I eventually derived the advantages that came from being among the first movers in the fast-growing and highly profitable new field of private equity.

The term 'private equity' has come to be applied in imprecise ways, sometimes to include venture capital and at other times to be almost synonymous with buy-outs. As I use it, it takes in the whole spectrum of investment in unquoted shares: venture capital in new and early-stage companies; expansion capital in more established firms; buy-ins of under-managed firms requiring an injection of new management; and buy-outs of profitable companies of every size. In this book I have sometimes stressed the inclusion of early-stage investing by referring to the venture-capital and private-equity industry.

There have always been privately financed companies. Private equity existed in fourteenth- and fifteenth-century Italy, where merchant bankers would fund enterprise and trade. In the sixteenth and seventeenth centuries, when European traders were travelling to the New World and the Far East, voyages were funded by private investors, each of whom took a share of the risk and a share of the profits in proportion to his or her investment. By custom, the captain of the ship took 20 per cent of the value of the cargo. That rule still applies: private-equity firms generally take a carried interest of 20 per cent of the capital gain made by the funds under their management. Then in the nineteenth century there were the private banks, Barings, Rothschilds and others, who were funding private businesses.

The difference today is that the private-equity industry is not run by ships' captains or bankers but by firms for whom private-equity investment is a profession. Our skill lies in our long-term professional approach to taking business risk. We raise funds, almost entirely from pension funds and institutional investors; we identify companies in which to invest those funds; we take large enough shareholdings to have real influence over the companies' affairs; we have a clear strategy in view for growth and for exit; we strengthen the boards and executive teams of the companies in which we invest; and we make resources available for strategic initiatives. Unlike the public-company model (that is, the model of companies listed on a public stock exchange), in which shareholders are a long way removed from operational and even strategic issues, the private-equity model is one of close involvement by empowered, expert investors. It is a model of turning employee-managers into owners of their businesses and of adding value through active ownership.

In performing this function, the private-equity industry as a whole has outperformed the stock markets in the United States, Europe and the Far East for the past decade, while the best and longest-established firms in the industry have outperformed the markets for two decades or more.

When the two partners dropped out of MMG, and Maurice Tchénio told me that he would prefer to operate more independently, I knew that I would not succeed if I tried to build such a business without an international dimension, basing it in London only. It was clear to me that the United States, not France, was the crucial piece of the puzzle, because business, finance and venture-capital activity was much more developed in the United States than it was in Europe. What I needed in order to reverse the difficult turn of events was to find a new partner in New York, not Chicago, where our erstwhile American partner had been based. Whom did I know in New York who could replace our departing partner?

I was chatting about this with my mother, who is herself entre-preneurially minded, when the answer came to me: Alan Patricof.

I had met Alan a couple of years previously and we had got on extremely well. The chemistry was right. We are still close friends now, more than thirty years later. He was one of the pioneers of American venture capital. He had set out a few years before me, in 1969, when he raised a $2.5 million fund from wealthy individuals in the United States. Among his investors were two leading figures in American business, Bob Sarnoff and Edgar Bronfman. He had also set up a corporate-finance advisory business to supplement the rev-enues of his venture fund.

I telephoned Alan and made him an offer: 'Our Chicago-based partner is leaving. If you want to become our partner, we could help you in corporate finance in the United States and you could help us to bring venture capital to Europe.' Alan is the most careful of people; he does not often make commitments on the phone. But on this occasion he immediately said yes. We soon agreed on a fee-sharing arrangement for the corporate-finance business we would do initially, and the deal was done.

MMG continued as an advisory business, with a New York office for which Alan was responsible. Our London office was to become the British arm of the expanded private-equity firm, Alan Patricof Associates, when we raised our first venture-capital fund in 1981. The French office, under Maurice Tchénio, likewise used the Alan Patricof name when it raised its first venture-capital fund in 1983. The names MMG and Alan Patricof Associates co-existed for some years, then we changed the name to MMG Patricof and finally, in 1991, as the firm expanded geographically and we felt the need to create a unified, international brand, the name in Europe was changed to Apax Partners.

Shortly after signing the agreement with Alan and his partner Bob Faris, who also became my good friend, I received a telephone call from Richard Frank, founder of Lawry's Foods in the United States. I had helped Richard sort out a thorny acquisition Lawry's had previously made in the spice business in France. He had now decided to sell Lawry's and he wanted to hire me to advise him. The choice, he told me, had come down to me or the giant investment bank Goldman Sachs. He knew he was giving me a break, but he thought I would do a good job.

Richard was living proof that you can be 100 per cent a gentleman and 100 per cent ethical and still be a great financial success. Richard's father owned a famous steak house in Los Angeles, Lawry's Prime Rib. Frank senior prepared his own seasoning for the beef. It was so popular that customers were stealing the shakers from the tables to take home. Richard asked his father if he could take the seasoning and try to build it into a major brand. Lawry's Seasoned Salt, as it is called, is now an icon in the United States.

When we eventually closed the transaction, selling the company to Lipton, part of Unilever, for about $70 million (a lot of money in those days), I earned a substantial corporate finance fee, about $550,000.

I went to Alan Patricof with a cheque for one-third of the fee. Alan said, 'I cannot accept this. I did nothing.' But I insisted, 'That is the deal. That is what is due to you under our agreement.' Alan and Bob Faris had contributed nothing to the transaction and our partnership had hardly gotten under way, but it was what we had agreed. Alan has never forgotten it.

Clients like Lawry's Foods were valuable, but the assignments were purely advisory; with the benefit of Alan Patricof's example in the United States, we set our sights on being venture-capital investors. But since there was no venture-capital industry in Europe, and since none of the financial institutions, whether they were investment funds, lending banks or investment banks, really knew anything about early-stage businesses or buy-outs, we found that we had to get the venture-capital industry going ourselves.

In this respect we were no different from many of the current generation of entrepreneurs who start new firms in a new industry: you find that considerable effort is needed to build up the sector at the same time as you build up your firm. A lot of my energy went into making the case for venture capital. Some of my colleagues thought it was a waste of my time. But I did not think we could be successful without this effort. I was not the only one to realize it: some of our competitors recognized the same necessity. Among those who were very active in those early years were Michael Stoddart of Electra; Sir David Cooksey, Tony Lorenz, Colin Clive and Lionel Anthony, who were chairmen of the British Venture Capital Association (BVCA); Dick Onians, who was chairman of the European Venture Capital Association (EVCA); Roger Brooke of Candover; and Nick Ferguson of Schroder Ventures.

We organized meetings where we could pitch the case for venture capital to prospective investors. The first such meeting was held in London, at the Grosvenor House Hotel, in 1977. William Casey, the head of the Securities and Exchange Commission, which regulates US stock exchanges, spoke. He had been invited by Alan Patricof, who was also a speaker. Leading financial institutions came; but nobody was really interested in investing in small businesses. Private equity, venture capital, small-company investments: these were not on the agenda at that time. We persisted nevertheless, and in the early 1980s we organized annual forums in hotel conference halls at each of which about thirty entrepreneurs would stand up one after another to expound, in four minutes each, the virtues of their businesses to potential investors. We began to create a feeling that perhaps there were worthwhile entrepreneurs and ventures in Britain after all.

Coming out of one of these meetings, John McGregor (now Lord McGregor), then the Conservative Minister of Transport and a former director of the merchant bank Hill Samuel, took me aside and said: 'You're not going to get anywhere unless you form an organization that represents you. You have to have one, official voice.' That was the origin of both the BVCA, of which I was a founding director and the third chairman, and, later, the EVCA, in which I also played a founding role as a director.

Apax went on to have an exceptional track record in helping to build the sector. While I was there, the firm provided three chairmen of the BVCA: Adrian Beecroft followed me after a few years, and then Clive Sherling. We provided one of the founders, Maurice Tchénio, and one chairman, Patrick di Giovanni, of the BVCA's French equivalent, the Association Française des Investisseurs en Capital, AFIC. We provided one chairman of the European Venture Capital Association, Max Burger-Calderon. And the contribution has continued since my departure with the election of Eddie Misrahi as chairman of AFIC in 2007.

Thus, we built up the sector while building up our business.

By the end of the 1970s, I knew that we had to move away from the business model of providing corporate-finance advice and raising private placements of capital for one venture at a time. It was just too difficult. I wanted to follow Alan Patricof's lead and raise large funds from institutions – funds that we could invest at our discretion in a number of different ventures over a relatively long period of time, in the process earning management fees and a share of the increase in the funds' values (the 20 per cent interest, which investors in the fund 'carry' for the fund's managers). That was what was already happening in the United States. It was the business model to aim for.

In stark contrast to the USA, however, conditions in Europe did not favour entrepreneurship. Entrepreneurship requires an enabling environment, including low rates of tax on capital gains, supportive stock markets and policy initiatives to support enterprise and small businesses, such as only governments can provide. There was no such environment in Britain or any other European country.

As a keen observer of the United States, and with the benefit of Alan's experience, I had come to the conclusion that it would be impossible for us to raise a British venture-capital fund so long as there did not exist a stock market on which young companies could float with ease. American institutional investors would be crucial to the success of our fund-raising and their experience in the US had underlined the importance of a stock market like Nasdaq.

The reason for this, as I will explain in detail in the last chapter, is that appropriate stock markets significantly reduce the risk profile of early-stage investment: through flotations they shorten the period during which private-equity investors are at risk and they provide funding alongside private-equity investors in order to take young companies through to profitability.

Conditions suddenly improved when Margaret Thatcher became Prime Minister in 1979. Her administration brought down the highest rate of personal taxation to 40 per cent, which led a significant change of sentiment in Britain, away from a 'nine-to-five' mentality towards appreciation of the value of hard work. Shortly after that, the London Stock Exchange (LSE) introduced a 'junior' market, the Unlisted Securities Market (USM), for which we in the nascent venture-capital industry had long been clamouring. The creation of the USM was the missing component that made it possible for us to raise our first British fund.

The USM was designed to become a market for high-growth companies that would not be eligible – mostly because they were still too small or did not yet have a record of consistent profitability – for the 'main list' of the LSE. It enabled these companies to raise capital by selling shares to the public and having those shares traded. This was crucial to the development of the venture-capital industry in Britain because it gave us an exit route for early-stage investments by way of flotations. For the investor, the exit is as important as the entrance.

Unfortunately, the USM did not last long. In 1992, in the depths of the recession, the LSE decided to close it down on the grounds that it was not sufficiently popular. This was as absurd as asking the banks to close because they were not lending in a deep recession. As a reaction to our protests about the closure of the USM, the LSE set up a task force, which recommended the formation of a Nasdaq-like market in London in parallel with the main list. The result was a compromise: the creation in 1993 of the Alternative Investment Market, AIM.

For various reasons, including its very light-touch regulation, AIM was unsatisfactory from the point of view of those supporting high-growth firms, and so, together with Jos Peeters, Stani Yassukovich, Andrew Beeson, my partners at Apax and others, I spent ten years trying to create Easdaq, a Nasdaq-like market in Europe that we set up in 1996 with the help of Nasdaq itself.

Easdaq was largely unsupported by the investment-banking community in Europe (which profited more from trading shares in fragmented, inefficient markets), and, after attracting about fifty companies, faltered at the time of the hi-tech bubble and was eventually absorbed by Nasdaq. It then became a victim of Nasdaq's international retrenchment following the regulatory difficulties that Nasdaq faced in its home market.

To this day, European hi-tech entrepreneurs are at a serious disadvantage to their American counterparts because there is no European equivalent of Nasdaq, a serious and viable market for early-stage companies. The consequences are that European investment in early-stage companies is about half the level in the United States – $11 billion against $26 billion in 2005 and about $20 billion against $31 billion in 2006 – and Europe has fallen far behind the United States in technological innovation.

On the day they announced the creation of the USM at the end of 1980, we pulled out all the stops to raise the £10 million ($18 million) APA Venture Capital Fund, our first fund in Britain and at that point the joint-largest fund ever raised in Europe. I was thirty-four years old and still four years away from establishing a stable business. But I knew when we raised that fund that I was on my way. Half the fund was raised from US investors with Alan Patricof's invaluable help. The other half was raised in the United Kingdom with the help of Sir Alcon Copisarow. Alcon had been a successful director of McKinsey when I was there. He became the chairman of the first two funds we raised in Britain. It was he who introduced us to our brokers, Phillips and Drew.

When you launch your venture, you must be aware of the circumstances in which you are operating; you must know which factors are in your favour and which factors are likely to be obstacles in your path. Your task as an entrepreneur is to use circumstances to your maximum advantage.

One such circumstance for me was the establishment of the United Securities Market (USM). Another, which was a key contributor to the eventual success of Apax and the venture-capital sector as a whole, was the intertwining of the sector with emerging technologies. Having first materialized around Boston and San Francisco in the late 1960s, hi-tech enterprise and venture capital supported each other's advance, like a double helix.

When the history of the last quarter of the twentieth century comes to be written, I have no doubt that an important chapter will be entitled 'The Age of Entrepreneurship and Innovation'. Few periods in history can compare: perhaps only the Renaissance and the thirty years spanning the last quarter of the nineteenth century and the first few years of the twentieth, when the telephone, electricity generation, the radio, the motor car and the aeroplane were invented and introduced. The industries based on these inventions drove growth in the twentieth century. Growth in the twenty-first century will be powered by the electronic microchip, the personal computer, the cellular phone and the Internet – and the parallel discoveries arising from research into DNA, cloning and the mapping of the human genome. Technologies converge to create unforeseen opportunities. You could not map the human genome without the computer, just as you could not build skyscrapers without the electricity needed to power the elevators that take people to the higher floors.

The exploitation of technological convergence since the 1970s has resulted in products and services – in information technology, communications, entertainment and life sciences – that have transformed our lives. In the process, these products and services have given rise to some of the greatest corporate success stories in history.

For a brief period, the technology boom also fostered a host of ventures that promised more than they could deliver. This was the period of the hi-tech bubble, which brought thirty years of hi-tech growth and innovation to what threatened to be a sticky end.

Today, nobody likes to recall the hi-tech bubble. As an investor, it was an amazing episode to live through. There was an extraordinary explosion of technology-driven innovation and enterprise, much of it unconnected with any viable market. Anything that moved the application of technology forward or that provided a plausible dot.com service could go public at an exaggerated valuation. All of a sudden, instead of people in suits, people in jeans, sweaters and open-necked shirts came to us to raise money. Investment banks, seeking lucrative flotation work, were calling us every day to see what possible flotations lay in our portfolio.

That was the time when venture capitalists really were themselves in demand: we had become sellers, not buyers. Between 1995 and 2001, Apax took fifty-two companies public on the stock exchanges of Europe and the United States: averaging one flotation every six weeks for six years. In one way it was exhilarating; in another, it became a cause for increasing concern.

In the event, we were fortunate. We disposed of our hi-tech holdings just before the bubble burst in early 2000. In fact, we made seven times our money – about £1 billion – in our 1995 fund, which had a lot of hi-tech companies in its portfolio.

Venture capital, growth stock markets and new technology were important factors in the development of private equity in Europe as well as the United States. They were crucial to the evolution of Apax and to the eventual success of my own career. But they were not the only factors. There was one further element: buy-outs.

Buy-outs have propelled the private-equity industry into a position of prominence in the public eye, mostly because recent transactions have involved huge firms that are household names.

In the private-equity industry, we have had the ability, since the mid-1980s, to acquire established and profitable but nevertheless under-performing companies at reasonable prices, with our equity leveraged by debt. While this might appear to be very different from investing in early-stage companies, the general skills and disciplines of private equity are, in fact, applicable to both, the main difference being that skills in financial structuring are essential in buy-outs but irrelevant for early-stage companies.

At the outset, the size of buy-out targets was limited by the amount of equity that private-equity funds could invest and by the amount of bank debt that could be raised. Targets were mostly privately owned companies or subsidiaries of publicly traded companies. Today, with far more capital available to the private-equity industry, target companies can be quoted or private, and there is virtually no company that is too big to be considered.

Given that the high level of competition between private-equity firms has driven acquisition prices to historic highs, the value-added approach taken by the private-equity investor prevails more than ever today.

How do buy-outs work? The private-equity investor removes the company from public ownership, takes shareholder control, and offers ownership of a stake to management through whom it applies the same disciplines that it would to any venture-capital investment: it puts experienced people, usually its own, on the board; the business plan is critically re-examined and turbo-charged to get a higher level of performance; management is granted powerful financial incentives and strengthened if necessary; decision-making is stream-lined; and capital is made available for strategic initiatives. The aim is to improve growth and profitability, and eventually to sell the company to a strategic buyer or re-float it on the stock market.

For the investor, buy-outs have significant attractions compared with early-stage investments. The amounts of money involved are much larger, the companies are well established, they are easier to borrow against, and they more easily attract high-calibre management if that is required. The downside with buy-outs is that it is impossible to make the kind of percentage returns, or the multiples of the investment, that are achieved by successful early-stage investments.

As an example, at the time of writing Apax has just agreed the sale of its stake in Healthcare At Home, a virtual start-up when we invested in it thirteen years ago. We have achieved more than forty

"A DUEL? I'M NOT SURE WE
WOULD AGREE TO THAT BEING
PART OF THE BIDDING PROCESS."

By 2001, buy-outs were routinely put up for auction by investment
banks, and private-equity firms bid against each other aggressively.
Our Christmas card that year drew attention to the intensity of the
competition for buy-out opportunities.

times our total investment to make £100 million profit. This kind of performance cannot be matched by a buy-out.

But a smaller percentage return on a large investment can still add up to much more money than a large percentage return on a small investment. And with buy-outs, the number of companies that fail is much smaller than with young companies. Thus, while individually a buy-out cannot match the returns on a successful early-stage venture – such as Healthcare At Home or the hi-tech data solutions company Autonomy, on which we made more than 300 times our money on an investment of £1.47 million (about $2.5 million) – across a whole portfolio, buy-outs will give a more consistent overall return than early-stage investments, on much greater invested capital. This is especially true in Europe, where early-stage investment has proved very challenging.

As the European buy-out business developed, Apax launched balanced funds that invested across the whole spectrum from early-stage to big buy-outs in our chosen sectors: telecoms, information technology, healthcare, media, consumer products and retailing, and, later, financial services. We persuaded outstanding executives from these sectors to join our team. By 1990, eighteen years after MMG came into being, we had created a significant business.

Mrs Thatcher had opened the door to venture capital and private equity in Britain in 1979. However, for all the pro-entrepreneur sentiments of Mrs Thatcher's successive chancellors of the exchequer, they did little actually to promote entrepreneurial investment. Certainly, the Thatcher era left Britain with a far better business culture than before, and with lower levels of income tax, but we were still saddled with very high rates of capital gains tax, an unclear position about the role and status of entrepreneurs, and uncertainty about whether British financial institutions should invest in venture capital and private-equity funds.

It was Tony Blair's Labour government, which came to power in 1997, which gave the sector its biggest boost. Tony Blair spoke up in favour of institutional investment in private equity. In 1998, chancellor of the exchequer Gordon Brown reduced capital gains tax on business assets from 40 per cent to 10 per cent, which gave an immediate positive signal to enterprise. He appointed the respected City figure Paul Myners to look at institutional investment in private equity, resulting in a positive transformation of British institutions' understanding of the sector. Gordon Brown did this as part of a clear strategy to make the British economy more entrepreneurial, competitive and capable of steady growth and full employment.

Today, private-equity funds account for roughly $1.5 trillion of investment capacity (if we include debt, leveraged to equity at about 2:1), compared with over $40 trillion value of stock market capitalization across the world. So private equity represents less than 4 per cent of the value of quoted shares.

By every significant measure – growth, employment, investment, productivity and profitability – private equity has outperformed the publicly quoted market by a substantial margin. If that margin is reduced in future, it will be because private equity has provided a new yardstick by which to measure performance and this is having a galvanizing effect on the publicly quoted sector, so that publicly quoted companies are beginning to copy private equity's methods.

In private equity, the interests of the company, its management, the private-equity fund managers and the private-equity fund investors are all in alignment. In the public-company model, the interests of management and shareholders are all too often in conflict.

Despite its achievements, or perhaps because of them, private equity has recently come under attack in the United States and Europe, especially in Germany, Denmark and Britain. In 2005, Franz Münterfering, chairman of Germany's then ruling party, the Social Democrats, referred to private-equity fund managers as 'locusts'. He published a 'locust list' naming twelve companies, including Apax, who, he alleged, were destroying the German economy. In Britain, meanwhile, trade union officials and journalists have focused on the tax incentives available to private-equity fund managers and the wealth they have earned to attack the industry. In Europe, much more than in the United States, where a similar debate is taking place, the argument about wealth creation has often been influenced more by envy than by admiration of commercial success. This is not a sound basis for public policy, which needs to provide significant incentives for entrepreneurial risk-taking and the creation of new businesses that are crucial to a competitive economy aspiring to maintain full employment.

Anyone old enough to remember the economic climate in the 1970s will know that there has been a massive improvement in the world of enterprise and business since then, and that the benefits have been widely, if not universally, shared. Private equity can be proud to have been a significant contributor to that improvement.

In 2005, $232 billion of private-equity funds were raised around the world, 52 per cent in North America, 38 per cent in Europe and 8 per cent in the Asia-Pacific region. This is the same wave that started in the United States back in 1968. In my view, the wave will continue to build. It is possible to imagine private equity's leveraged investment increasing significantly beyond 10 per cent of stock market capitalization from its current level of around 4 per cent, particularly as the companies involved in buy-outs get larger and the line between publicly-owned and privately-owned companies gets increasingly blurred.

In the fifteen years to my departure from Apax, the funds for which I was responsible achieved an average rate of return for our investors of more than 30 per cent, net of all fees and carried interest (Apax earns fees for managing the funds as well as taking its 20 per cent share of the profits of the funds).

Over three decades, we invested in more than 350 ventures, ranging from biotechnology to bookselling. For every investment we made, we probably gave detailed consideration to fifty business plans. That means that we examined more than 15,000 plans in total: 500 or so plans a year, ten opportunities every week. By the time I left the firm in 2005, we had floated more than seventy companies, with combined initial public valuations of $34 billion. Many more companies were sold on to trade buyers or to other private-equity investors.

Our first institutional fund in the United States was launched by Alan Patricof in 1980 and raised just over $25 million, mainly from American pension funds. Alan was to lead our successful investments in AOL, Apple and other fast-growing companies in the United States. The following year, our first UK fund raised £10 million ($18 million). Thereafter we raised a further twenty-six funds in Europe, the United States, Israel and Japan. Some were national funds, some were regional funds and, especially in more recent years, some were global funds. The last two funds before I left Apax were launched in 2001 and 2005. They raised more than $5 billion each. When I left I had no doubt that Apax would go on to raise even larger funds in the future. Apax duly raised more than $14 billion for its 2007 fund.

With a mix of early-stage investments and buy-outs, Apax backed all kinds of businesses: global brands such as Apple and AOL; fashion labels Tommy Hilfiger and Calvin Klein; and satellite giants such as Inmarsat. Apax funds invested in the television network Kabel Deutschland and alternative energy company Q-Cell in Germany, Italian investment firm Azimut, French cosmetics retailer Sephora, bakery firm Panrico in Spain, Israeli telecommunications operator Bezeq, medical dressings company Mölnlycke in Scandinavia, Dutch newspaper group PCM Uitgevers and Romanian mobile phone operator Mobifon. In Britain, Apax funds invested in the currency exchange firm Travelex, Waterstone's bookstores, IT provider Computacenter, Autonomy, New Covent Garden Soup, the New Look fashion chain, Virgin Radio, the Yell and Thompson directories businesses, and Easy Everything.

Apart from the bioscience venture PPL Therapeutics, which created Dolly the cloned sheep, which could end up being one of the major technological breakthroughs of our time, the companies we have backed probably have not individually influenced the course of history. Collectively, however, they have certainly helped change the face of European and American business.

What has my experience taught me? First, that it is possible to climb the North Face. Indeed, we had no choice but to climb the North Face in order to build Apax. We had to move the fundamental prejudice against wealth-creation and risk-taking that existed in Europe thirty or more years ago. In those days, many people thought it was in the nature of the British, the Germans and the French not to take risks and not to be entrepreneurial. That has changed. The transformation of attitudes is far from complete but the reality is – and this is the second lesson that my experience has taught me – that almost everybody would like to make capital if given a real chance to do so.

A proportionately greater number of Europeans than Americans may decide they do not want to make the effort that is required in creating capital, or that job security is more important, but fundamentally there is now little difference between an American and a European entrepreneur, even if, despite the huge increase in their numbers in recent years, there are still far fewer entrepreneurs in Europe than in the United States.

This transformation of attitudes towards enterprise has been helped by the vicissitudes of large companies, which have shed jobs and can no longer hold out the prospect of lifetime careers for their employees. Some of the largest and most respected firms of thirty years ago have disappeared completely. US Steel, American Tobacco, International Harvester, Pan-Am and Sears were once among the giants of American business. Neither ICI, once Britain's biggest industrial company, which long ago de-merged its drugs business and reduced the scale of its chemicals and paints divisions, nor Rolls Royce, which went bust, reorganized, sold off its motorcar interests and now focuses on aero engines, exists today in the size or form it did thirty years ago.

International Business Machines (IBM), which once straddled the world like a colossus, has been overtaken by one of its former sub-contractors, Microsoft, which supplied the operating system for IBM's personal computers – a business from which IBM, unable to compete with Dell, Compaq and others, subsequently withdrew. Texaco, at one time the only oil company to sell fuel to the public in every state in the United States, got into difficulties in the mid-1980s, sold off many of its businesses and entered into various capital-saving joint ventures before succumbing to a takeover by Chevron in

2001. In Europe, the giant Dutch consumer electronics manufacturer Philips endured a two-decade roller-coaster ride, shedding thousands of jobs along the way.

The debate about job destruction and job creation, and their respective impacts on overall employment, productivity and economic growth, is one that preoccupies economists and social scientists. It is clear, however, that, especially in the United States, as economies have moved from a reliance on smokestack industries to technology and services, there has been a 'push' away from job security in large companies as well as a 'pull' towards entrepreneurship and employment in both large and small growth companies. It is estimated that in the United States sixty million jobs have been created by new firms in the past thirty years, while fifty million jobs have been lost by established companies.

By the time I stood down from the chairmanship in August 2005, Apax itself had more than three hundred employees, and offices in London, New York, Silicon Valley, Munich, Paris, Milan, Madrid, Stockholm and Tel Aviv. We had more than $20 billion under management – when $20 billion was still thought to be a lot of money!

The greatest challenge in Alpine mountaineering is the North Face of the Eiger. Those who have climbed it are recognized as the best. My partners and I felt we had climbed the North Face.

What lessons can you draw from my personal story? First, that you must find an opportunity that matches your skills and ambition. When I started out there were opportunities in hi-tech, but I am not a hi-tech person. I could not have built an Intel or a Google. Had I stayed at McKinsey I would have been able to use my analytical skills in calibrating the strengths and weaknesses of companies, identifying their best opportunities and putting in place the structures to take advantage of those opportunities, but it would not have satisfied my ambition. The opportunity that suited me – that used my skills and satisfied my ambition – was the opportunity to bring money and enterprise together. Even at the age of twenty-six you can quite easily identify what suits your skills and ambition.

Second, your business will grow to match the size of your vision. Once you have decided on the business you want to build, fixing the vision is the biggest constraint on the scale of your future success. I could have worked entirely in an advisory capacity, building the firm into a consultancy business. But that was not my vision. I could have stayed in the venture capital area, investing only in start-ups and early-stage ventures. Again, that was not my vision; I wanted to be bigger. I could have worked only in the UK, but I wanted to be international. Scale was important to my vision and I had to over-come all manner of obstacles and constraints to achieve it. Again, twenty-six is not too young to gauge the scale of your vision.

Third, you have to understand the environment around you. When I started, the British economy was in a mess, taxation was high, and few investors were paying attention to entrepreneurs. This meant that my journey was going to be a long one. It took twelve years to get properly established in the private-equity business, with two venture-capital funds totalling £40 million. It took a further nine years for the size of the funds under our management to jump to billions of dollars. Apax's growth has followed an accelerating curve. I could not foresee that curve when I started out, but I could sense that the opportunity before me could be the Next Big Thing. I had to keep a close eye on circumstances, improve them where I could – for example, through the British Venture Capital Asso-ciation – and take advantage of positive changes, such as the increased dynamism that followed the reduction of corporate and capital gains tax rates and the launch of the USM, to push the business ahead.

I constantly sought to improve our chances by taking initiatives earlier than my competitors, by doing things that others would not do. I deliberately chose the North Face because I felt that it was the route to something really outstanding that few others would be tempted to try.

This speaks to the fourth lesson: perseverance. If you have matched the opportunity you have chosen to your skills and ambition and if you have a clear vision of your goal, you must stick with it. It might take years. Business involves a lot of hard grind. I could have abandoned my quest when two of my original partners dropped out in 1975. There were several moments thereafter when I could have said 'enough'. I did not. I stuck with it, confident that I would eventually reap the rewards.

The growth of enterprise is not going to come to an end any time soon. Doubtless there will be further serious corrections in the capital markets and these will reveal weaknesses in this or that sector, but overall it is reasonable to expect the entrepreneurial wave to continue building, and the private-equity wave with it.

Circumstances have improved dramatically for entrepreneurs since I started out in 1972. The global economy is growing, in many countries the tax regime now encourages risk-taking, and a much broader investment community is willing to back private-equity funds and good companies with good ideas.

This is a favourable time to be an entrepreneur. If you are one for whom the North Face is an exciting, even irresistible, challenge, aim high. The higher you aim, the higher you will go. This book will, I hope, help you get to the summit.

2

FEAR OF FAILURE

You can't learn
to swim by exercising
on the beach.

Whether entrepreneurship is for you depends on a number of factors, the first of which is your attitude towards risk.

Risk is an emotive word that masks the value of uncertainty. The difference between risk and uncertainty is one of personal perception as much as substance. Risk-takers are commonly thought to be rash and impulsive. Risk has the connotation of danger. Indeed, the word risk is derived from the Italian *rischiare*, which means to run into danger. Uncertainty, on the other hand, suggests only that there is insufficient knowledge to be able to predict the outcome or to assess accurately the chances, or the value, of success. By and large, when discussing entrepreneurship, it is more constructive to talk about uncertainty than to talk about risk, if only because the word risk provokes such a negative emotional reaction.

Uncertainty and opportunity, as I have explained, go together; indeed, the first task of the entrepreneur is to seek out opportunity in uncertainty. The approach to uncertainty taken by most people is conditioned by two opposing drives: their ambition to achieve success and their personal anxiety about failure. But successful entrepreneurs are not like most people: they do not fear failure. By this I do not mean that entrepreneurs do not believe they can fail. I mean, on the contrary, that entrepreneurs know that failure is part of the process and they are not afraid of it. They know that if they persevere they will eventually succeed, despite setbacks along the way.

Can your attitudes towards uncertainty and failure be changed by reading a book? Possibly not. Perhaps the best we can hope for is that this chapter will help you define your personal attitude to risk and, in so doing, enable you to identify the role that you might play in an entrepreneurial venture. It might also help you recognize the key personal attributes of successful entrepreneurs.

Over the years, many potential entrepreneurs have come to my office looking for support at the start of their ventures. I have heard experienced executives say that they are considering leaving salaried employment to start their own firms. People working for large consultancy companies have come to me for advice about how to get a new business off the ground. I have had journalists and doctors in my office looking for new careers in business.

Recent years have seen many new entrepreneurs come out of the academic world into technology-led businesses, especially in the areas of information technology and life sciences. Others have moved from big-company environments into their own small, high-potential ventures, from coffee shops to search engines.

All of this is evidence that many more people than before are considering the entrepreneurial road. Perhaps you are one of them.

But the recent dramatic shift towards enterprise does not mean that everybody has the mindset of an entrepreneur.

I recently tried to recruit a partner for a new investment venture. I offered the candidate a package that gave him a substantial share of the performance of the investment funds he could participate in managing, and equity in the firm, as well as a guaranteed salary and bonus that were greater than in his current employment. He said he needed more and cited a figure that was far higher than we could possibly offer. He said, 'I cannot leave what I already have for anything less.'

What this person wanted was to be compensated far beyond the market rate for what he perceived to be a degree of insecurity. His message to me was that, although in principle he wanted the job, in practice he was not the person to take the risk.

I asked him if he valued security more than the rewards of success. He was taken aback. He had never thought of himself in those terms at all.

I then asked him what the venture would have to achieve for him to exceed his present remuneration on the basis of the package I had offered him. He quoted a revenue number. I asked, 'What do you think is the probability of getting to thirty per cent more than that level of revenue?' He replied, 'Seventy per cent.' At the higher level, the terms I had offered would have made him a reasonably wealthy man in a few years. If he really thought the chance of outstanding success was 70 per cent but was still not prepared to take the risk without enormous guaranteed compensation, there was only one conclusion: he wanted the rewards of entrepreneurial success without the uncertainty that goes with it.

This illustrates that our perceptions of uncertainty and risk are highly subjective. The candidate saw a 70 per cent chance of success

Risk is
an emotive word
that masks
the value
of uncertainty

as offering a high risk of failure for which he wanted higher guaranteed compensation. I would regard 70 per cent as offering a high probability of success.

This difference of perspective mirrors two basic approaches to any entrepreneurial opportunity: appreciation of the upside (how much profit it can make) and fear of the downside (how much it will cost if it fails). Depending on how secure and confident we are, we may overestimate or underestimate either prospect. Some people discount the downside: they just 'know' that their venture is going to be a success. Most err in the opposite direction.

Despite the positive shift in attitudes towards enterprise over the last thirty years, the pessimistic view is still common in Europe. Indeed, it sometimes seems as if Europeans are more preoccupied by the possibility of failure than the possibility of success: enterprise is perceived as a form of Trial by Ordeal – a test of guilt or innocence – which, if it goes the wrong way, reveals a basic personal flaw.

If somebody fails in Europe, the stigma can make it difficult to try again. In the United States there is a much healthier view, that enterprise is a process of Trial and Error: if your venture fails, people accept that the experience will stand you in good stead when you begin again. When I was starting out, I became friendly with an American entrepreneur who was on top of the world, with several beautiful homes and all he cared to own. He made a poor business decision, lost everything, became a taxi driver in New York, and then made a second fortune in a new venture. Friends came to his aid and investors did not hesitate to back him the second time. I and everyone around him sympathized with him at the time of his difficulties, and then admired him for overcoming his initial failure, starting a venture again from scratch and making a success of it.

It is important for you to know that there will be setbacks on the way to entrepreneurial success. Some will be your own responsibility: misreadings of the marketplace, wrong hirings, false starts, dead ends, ill-advised diversification, under-capitalization or overtrading. Others will be out of your hands: unexpected shifts in underlying economic conditions, volatile interest or exchange rates or sudden changes in the competitive environment. For a long time your venture might not thrive in the way you had hoped. But if you have what it takes to be an entrepreneur, you will know that the road ahead can be travelled even if the going gets tough. Not minding if you fail once or twice before you get it right – because that is the nature of the process – is a fundamental aspect of being an entrepreneur. You must have the confidence to use the lessons of setbacks – your own and other peoples' – to full advantage.

I have experienced setbacks in my own career, not only in terms of unsuccessful investments – of which there have inevitably been many – but in terms that threatened the very existence of my firm. Indeed, when two of my three partners dropped out of MMG in 1975 there was a real question about whether our venture would survive.

But I never doubted my chances of achieving eventual success, and I never worried about ultimate failure.

The degree to which you fear failure often reflects the values of the family you come from. This may have been the case with my hard-to-please job candidate, whose father, it turned out, was risk averse. There are many families where failure, whether at school or at work, is regarded as the worst thing that can happen. Sometimes this is an expression of timidity. In such a family, you do not set yourself up for a fall, you do not take risks. Instead, you apply yourself diligently to the achievement of respectable, but limited, goals. If you come from that type of family you are likely to be too conservative to decide easily to become an entrepreneur. In other cases, fear of failure reflects an inability to cope with the possibility of loss of face or rejection. Again, if you come from that type of family you might be too inhibited to be an entrepreneur.

If, by contrast, you come from a family where there has been an awareness of entrepreneurial success, where the discussion of risk has been part of everyday conversation, where setbacks have been overcome and where the possibility of a setback is regarded as part of the territory, it is more likely that you will have the confidence to become an entrepreneur.

Either way, personal circumstances have shaped your approach.

I have worked with successful colleagues who were constant worriers. I gave one of them a plate that to this day hangs on his wall. On it is written: 'Today is the tomorrow you worried about yesterday.' He was constantly worrying about what could go wrong in order to avoid it.

I would say to him: 'Not to worry, we can deal with it.' I, too, am conscious of what might go wrong, but it does not inhibit my confidence or ambition. I certainly have to stretch to achieve my objectives. If there are setbacks, I am always trying to turn them to advantage. In any event, I avoid the emotional roller-coaster. If something terrible happens and members of the team are downcast, the leader's job is to lift them up. You have to be able to inspire confidence in order to motivate. You cannot do so if you are in a state of high anxiety yourself and unsure of your ultimate success.

It is logical that immigrants are heavily represented among the ranks of successful entrepreneurs. They have to overcome hurdles in establishing themselves in their new countries and their initial success gives them confidence to go further. They take risks because they have done it before and they have succeeded. Initially, they may have very little to lose and they have an expectation that, as long as they apply themselves energetically to the task in hand and persevere, they will be successful.

My own professional life has probably been governed by three drivers. First, as an enforced emigrant from my homeland, I felt a powerful drive to prove myself. We lost everything in Egypt. Such an experience provides a powerful motor for ambition. My awareness of the need to provide for my parents probably had the same effect.

Second, I was successful academically. At school, I soon rose to the top of the class. At Oxford and Harvard I did well. This success was reinforced by the endorsement of my family and my teachers. The combination of my desire to succeed and my confidence in my ability to succeed drove me to be very ambitious.

The third driver was the environment provided by my family. My father was in business and my mother has a positive, entrepreneurial mindset, so the discussion of business issues, of risk, of entrepreneurial problems and opportunities, was the stuff of dinner-table conversation.

This combination of drivers pushed me towards a commercial career. I chose entrepreneurship rather than the security of a well-paid job because I was confident I could rise to the challenge.

I realized that, compared to most people, I have a powerful desire to achieve and an unusual capacity for hard work.

Many people would like to be successful in business and to leave the legacy of a great company behind them. But you have to ask yourself, deep down, do you think that you are cut out for the entrepreneurial life? Are you suited to living with the stress of uncertainty, of being responsible for the performance that pays your employees' (and your own) wages?

To answer these questions, it might be helpful to consider the personal qualities of those who have successfully travelled the entrepreneurial road before you. Matching your skills against theirs should give you a better sense of your aptitude for an entrepreneurial career.

The first set of characteristics that I have observed in the successful entrepreneurs backed by Apax over the last three decades is that they are good leaders, that they have an inspiring vision, and that they are able to attract and manage talented people. Leadership is a difficult quality to acquire: some have it, others do not.

The second set of characteristics is that they are driven to succeed and are obsessive about their businesses. Again, drive is a difficult quality to acquire: generally, you either have it or you do not.

Far more than most, they are persevering and capable of extraordinary effort to achieve their goals.

Invariably, they are self-confident, optimistic and competitive, and the microcosm of the world they have in their heads corresponds to reality.

In addition, they have some unusual talent for their chosen opportunity, as well as a deep fascination with it. As a consequence, they develop a deep understanding of their market and their business.

Most of all, successful entrepreneurs have an appetite for uncertainty, which is kept in check by an inclination to take calculated risks rather than to 'bet the shop'.

Few entrepreneurs I have met could identify with all these points, but probably every successful entrepreneur could put a tick beside most. It will not be exactly the same combination in every case, but it will be 60 per cent the same.

In my experience, successful entrepreneurs tend to be extreme personalities. In fact, the more extreme their personalities, the more ambitious they will be and the higher they will aim. Just as every person's perception of uncertainty is different, so every person's hunger for success is different. Having asked yourself if you are cut out for entrepreneurship, your second question is: 'How hungry am I? Am I prepared to devote myself wholeheartedly to the task of building a business?'

If you cannot answer 'yes' immediately, ambitious entrepreneurship is probably not for you.

Some successful entrepreneurs write books at the end of their careers in which they portray themselves as battling against all the odds and succeeding by a supreme effort of will and self-belief. But, if you look behind the bluster of those memoirs, you will nearly always find something much more calculated and better thought through than the image projected.

Most people do not appreciate that enterprise is a profession. If you have the fundamental personal attributes, the rest can be learned. Discerning what needs to be learned is the essence of this book.

You do not need to have been to university or business school to learn how to be successful as an entrepreneur. Being streetwise and hungry for success is just as important. There are many people who learn informally from life, from hardship. Many entrepreneurs left school at sixteen and had no education beyond that. They have learned to analyse, to make judgements and to make decisions. Their lives have made them highly educated in entrepreneurship.

But being self-taught is not the easiest launch pad. Far better to be educated if you have the chance. It is useful, also, to go to business school. What business school provides is accelerated experience. I could not have done what I did in my field as early as I did if I had not been to business school. That concentrated learning was reinforced by the two years I spent at McKinsey, which acted as a super business school for me. So if you have the opportunity to go to business school, take it. It will save you time.

It will also give you exposure, if you do not already have it, to the world of numbers and finance. Every business school graduate will sit examinations in finance, accounting information, quantitative methods and business economics. It is useful for entrepreneurs to be numerate and it is essential that you understand the cash flow and balance sheet, as well as the profit and loss account, of your venture. Without that understanding, you will be stumbling around.

It is sometimes said that for every successful entrepreneur there are 999 who fail, and that the difference between the successes and the failures is simply luck.

For every one who succeeds there are many who fail: that much is true. People give up. If they had not given up they might yet be successful. But the idea that it is a chance in a thousand that you will be successful is just another way of expressing fear of failure. Success is not a chance in a thousand. If entrepreneurs have some of the personal qualities listed above, if they know what they are good at and if they go about the task in the right way, the chances of success increase substantially.

How successful you become depends on your comfort zone in terms of achievement. Once you have reached that zone, you are unlikely to take further risks, partly for fear of losing what you have got.

Apax funds invested in the anti-virus software company, Dr Solomon's. Alan Solomon was the leader in the anti-virus software market, but he did not think he could go further with it and he wanted to sell out. He and his wife had built the company to the size they could manage. They did not enjoy the managerial challenge. From a purely entrepreneurial point of view, they probably did not push the business far enough. They did not stick with it long enough. They got out too early.

We floated the company on Easdaq at the end of 1996 and achieved an Initial Public Offering (IPO) value of $312 million. This was a great result, but, had they wanted to, they could have taken their company further.

It is my view that some of those who believe that success is a chance in a thousand, who attribute success to luck or who are prepared to settle for a moderate level of achievement, could do far better if they attached themselves to someone who has the entrepreneurial qualities they lack. Linking up with talented entrepreneurs does not necessarily relegate you to the ranks of the also-rans. It is simply a recognition – an accurate calibration – of what you personally need and what you can contribute. Entrepreneurs have weaknesses. Their success depends on the recruitment of outstandingly talented people who, in part, compensate for those weaknesses.

There is no disgrace in not being the leader, in being a member of an entrepreneurial team. The great thing about entrepreneurial companies is that – like sports teams – everybody helps to meet the challenge and everybody collects a share of the rewards and a share of the fulfilment. A good entrepreneur, aware of his or her own weaknesses, will be looking for such colleagues.

When is the right time to venture forth? I was twenty-six when I started my business. At the age of twenty-six you can afford to take risks that you cannot take so easily at the age of thirty-five and which you may not be able to take again until the age of fifty when your children have finished school and your appetite for risk returns.

Age is a very important factor. Entrepreneurship is demanding. It is not easy to start a venture when you have three children at school

"SHE CAN'T UNDERSTAND WHY OUR ANTI-VIRUS SOFTWARE
DIDN'T CURE HER COLD."

The flotation of Dr Solomon's gave us the theme for our 1997 Christmas card. We were very happy with the value we achieved when Dr Solomon's became Easdaq's first flotation in 1996. It was subsequently acquired by the American anti-virus software company Norton. Had management wanted, they could have taken the company further.

and a mortgage to pay. It might be easier when you have emerged from that, when you are older and have plenty of work experience.

While I do not discount the value of experience and maturity, my general advice is to start early rather than late. You are never going to be 100 per cent ready.

'You cannot learn to swim by exercising on the beach' is what I used to say to my two sceptical partners in the early days of MMG. If you start young, you have plenty of time in which to be successful; and to make, and learn from, mistakes. A danger of leaving it late is not just that you have less time, but that you will be too comfortable in your life ever to start.

Many people stop at the conceptual stage of their proposed venture and stay in salaried employment for another twenty years. We all know people like that: people who grasp the idea of entrepreneurship, but do not grasp an opportunity, either because they lack confidence or because they are settled in well-paid jobs and feel they have too much to lose. Or it could be that they never seriously get around to looking for an opportunity.

It takes a certain daring to get started on the entrepreneurial road and to travel it successfully; not foolhardiness, but daring to reach further than you can easily reach. Sometimes my colleagues at Apax wanted to go only so far and no further. I set the bar as high as I thought we could go. As soon as we reached it, I put the bar higher. Every time I put the bar higher, it required daring for the firm to excel. Every time you dare, there is a risk of failure. You dare because somewhere inside you know you can do it. Your self-confidence, your past track record, your previous success, all tell you that it can be done.

Anyway, what is the worst that can happen? If you fail, you will learn from that failure and it will stand you in good stead when you start again. Yes, sometimes people are ruined by failure, but that is a rare outcome and when it happens there is usually some other element of misfortune or foolishness involved.

Tom Judge of the AT&T pension fund was one of the earliest supporters of venture capital in both the United States and Europe; he was, fortunately for us, one of the earliest investors in Apax funds. So important was his participation in a fund that if he was in, other investors would follow. If he stayed out, they stayed out. He was considered the doyen of institutional investors during his fifteen years at AT&T's pension fund, years in which he created a venture-capital portfolio that grew from zero to $1.5 billion and returned on average 25 per cent per year. He was, in the American parlance, a smart investor.

I remember Tom saying to me in the early 1980s that there are certain areas of investment, like private equity, where you need faith. You need to understand all the reasons why the investment should work out, and then you need faith. The same is true of entrepreneurs: entrepreneurs need faith in themselves and in their ventures.

If you set out on the entrepreneurial road, how likely is it that you will be successful? Subsequent chapters of this book look at the key variables in the success of an entrepreneurial business. For the present, I want to focus on the personal element: the impact of each individual entrepreneur on the probability of success.

At Apax, we turned down the opportunity to invest in the business of the domestic-appliance entrepreneur James Dyson. Dyson became a huge success. By 2005, his company had grown to £400 million of sales and £100 million of pre-tax profits. It was clear when he came to us that he personally had many of the key entrepreneurial qualities. We thought, however, that he was taking on something that was extremely difficult: to challenge the massive incumbents – Hoover, Miele, AEG, Electrolux and Bosch – in the mature market of domestic appliances; a market in which there were significant barriers to entry, not least in terms of the costs of product development, manufacturing, distribution, marketing and brand awareness.

What is more, Dyson was not intending to compete on price; he aimed to compete on design and technological innovation. We thought the chances of success were small. In this, we made a mistake. We underestimated the effectiveness of Dyson's marketing as much as we underestimated the design appeal and efficiency of his products. Most of all, we underestimated Dyson himself. He made the difference.

It is always good to be reminded that just because something is unlikely to happen it does not mean that it will not happen. Even low-probability events, by definition, do occur. Just because James Dyson's venture seemed to us to have a low probability of success did not mean that it would not be successful.

At Apax we were not trying to invest in every single entrepreneur who was going to be successful. What we were trying to do was to have a good record of success. That meant excluding those who had a high probability of failure, even if some of them subsequently were to prove successful. Because you take certain risks and they work out, it does not mean that those risks were reasonable risks to take. A risk with a high probability of failure is not a risk worth taking, even if high probability of failure is not certainty of failure. A lottery ticket has a high probability of failure, but every week one person succeeds. Apax would avoid ventures that had a high probability of failure, despite the knowledge that some of them might succeed.

Probability is not a tangible thing. You do not know even after the event whether the degree of probability that you ascribed to an opportunity was right or wrong. Your judgement can only be tested if you have very similar occurrences over a long period of time. Dyson's decision to forge ahead reflected his confidence in himself and in his venture. We believed it had a high probability of failure; he did not agree.

Having said that, probability, unlike beauty, is not merely in the eyes of the beholder. Developing an objective judgement about what is likely to work is important. The nineteenth-century British prime minister Benjamin Disraeli said that politics was the art of the possible. I like to say that venture capital is the art of the *seemingly* impossible. It is not that you think there is one chance in a hundred and you happen to be lucky, it is that you perceive the chance to be far better than 50/50. It is the man in the street who perceives it to be one in a hundred. When, as a private-equity investor, you have a successful investment, it is not a matter of luck. It is the result of an informed decision. You have gauged the probability correctly.

Unless they have been to business school, or are of a mathematical bent, most people do not think in terms of probabilities. A person looking at two opportunities will be drawn to examine the upside and the downside of each. If this one works, it can make $100; if the other one works it can make $60. If the downside is the same in both cases, the one that can make $100 looks more attractive. That judgement does not take probability into account. Probability might say that the first opportunity, if it works, can make $100 but the probability of it working is only 10 per cent, whereas the second opportunity, which has an upside of only $60, has a probability of 60 per cent. Seen in that perspective, the second is far more attractive.

Entrepreneurs are dealing with probability all the time without even realizing it. The product, price, team, market, financial expertise, sales, marketing and technology: each of these has a probability factor, a probability of being able to deliver. Arriving at a blended probability for the venture as a whole is an exercise of judgement that requires a grasp of what is likely to happen on multiple fronts. A multiplicity of second bounces has to be taken into account and integrated into a workable plan.

Many people choose to fly by the seat of their pants. They are seduced by the magnitude of the prospective reward, but do not have a deep understanding of the likelihood of their venture's success. By contrast, great entrepreneurs have a grasp of probability that has been highly tuned by their personal experience. They know better than most what it is realistic to expect.

One of the images that had currency in the private-equity business in the early years was that of fairground hoops. The probability of getting the hoop on the tenth peg was obviously less than the probability of getting it on the first peg. When we were investing in early-stage companies, we decided that we were not going to aim for the tenth peg; at best we were going to aim for the seventh peg.

Sometimes, if your life depends on it, you can throw a hoop and it does fall on the tenth peg. It is not just luck; it is also the adrenalin that sharpens your skills. There is something in that. I do think that your personal skills and determination have a strong influence on probability. Sometimes you will hear a management team talking about the way their firm should move forward, and people will say 'We can't do this' and 'We can't do that', and then someone else steps forward to take the leadership role and says, 'If we really set our mind to this, we can pull it off. Let us just set our minds to it.' I think you do, as a venture capitalist or as an entrepreneur, through force of will, achieve difficult things. You do not bend events to your will, that is impossible. But through force of will, you drive the achievement of your objective despite all the obstacles in the way.

Conquering the North Face is certainly harder than going up the easier route. But the probability of your being able to conquer the North Face depends upon you. You are the difference. Gauging this type of probability is essentially a matter of personal perception.

Ernest Shackleton went to the South Pole in 1915. The whole enterprise was poorly planned. His ship, appropriately named *Endurance*, was frozen into the ice. He and his men tried to drag three small boats across Antarctica but had to give up. They trekked back across the ice and then rowed to a barren island. Shackleton went off in one of the rowing boats with two of the men and travelled 800 miles across the worst seas in the world – waves up to a mile long and ninety feet high. They made it to South Georgia, but landed on the wrong side of the island. They tried to cross the mountain range in the centre of the island three times. The third time they made it. Shackleton got a ship and went back to rescue his men. He failed. It took four attempts on four ships before he achieved success. His motto was: 'Through endurance, we succeed.'

You could fault Shackleton on the basis that had he been a wiser explorer he would have learned from Captain Scott (whom Shackleton had accompanied on a previous expedition) and Roald Amundsen (who had won the race to be first to the South Pole) about what was and was not possible. He should have known that he needed two ships, so that if one got ice-bound, the other would still be available. Had he planned it correctly, he would not have had all his problems. But the feat that he accomplished in the end, returning with all his men alive, was certainly greater than that of crossing the South Pole.

No one has done anything like it before or since.

Here you had a man who was determined to succeed. He had great qualities of leadership and led from the front. His men slept, he did not. With those qualities of endurance, perseverance and leadership, Shackleton's chances of success – the probability of his being able to rescue all his men – were far higher than they would have been for anybody else. The ability to get yourself out of difficult situations and to persuade others to trust you is an essential ingredient in the probability of success. You look at one person and you would not trust him to achieve a certain goal, but you would trust another. Or you might trust that person to achieve a different goal.

Probability in business is not verifiable in the way it is for a lottery ticket. It is dependent upon the characters of the people involved, the nature of the opportunity and the challenges of the business plan.

With the benefit of my experience, I can say that probably 80 per cent of the ventures in which I invest will be successful to some degree. What I cannot say is the extent to which each will be successful. We did not know that Mike Lynch of Autonomy would make $750 million for us when we first invested in his company. That would have been impossible to predict. What I did know, however, was that he was a terrific entrepreneur, and that he was likely to go much further than his business plan predicted. Anyone who could persuade someone in a pub to lend him £2,000 to start a business was likely to go far. Once he had shown he could build up the business profitably from year to year, it was clear he would be highly successful. He was a person to back.

As a venture capitalist, you expect to lose money on 20 per cent of the companies in which you invest, not 50 per cent or 80 per cent. You also know that you seldom find somebody totally surprising being hugely successful. You take people through this sieve – the disciplined process of due diligence and business planning – and you end up with some good jockeys starting the race.

Stop worrying about failure and put that energy into winning the race

I remember visiting Richard Branson on his houseboat in Little Venice, in West London, in the 1970s. Young as he then was, he had absolute faith in his own ability. He was sure he would succeed. Many years later, the radio disc jockey Chris Evans came to see us, wanting funds with which to buy Virgin Radio. He was thirty years old with no previous business experience, but he had tremendous faith that he could make it work. We backed him in acquiring Virgin Radio for £180 million and he did make it work. We backed Sir Stelios Haji-Ioannou, the founder of EasyJet and multiple entrepreneur, in his venture Easy Everything. Again, he was an entrepreneur who set his sights high and had a clear sense of what he could achieve. All three had enormous self-confidence.

There is, inevitably, a feeling of trepidation when you start out; but it is the sort of trepidation you feel when you get on to the track for a race. You know what you can do. The nerves are just the adrenalin. You need the nerves to perform at your best.

The principal task of the entrepreneur is to seek out the opportunity offered by uncertainty and take advantage of it. Where there is uncertainty, there is the possibility of great success.

So long as you are frightened by the prospect of failure, you will probably not get started, and even if you do get started you will not go as far as you would if you were less troubled by fear. You have to have faith in your own ability to succeed, both in order to start and in order to go far.

My advice is: stop worrying about failure. It causes grave anxiety and consumes a lot of energy. Put that energy into winning the race.

3

CALIBRATING OPPORTUNITIES

If you pick a provincial line, you arrive at a provincial destination.

Many people want to be in business but have no idea what business to be in. Most commonly, they think they need a brilliant new idea, like the iPod; that they need to create a new market with a new product or a new technology. Some businesses are built on that basis, but most are not. Plenty of successful businesses are built on delivering a conventional product or service in a more efficient way.

The courier company Fedex took an existing business sector and offered a much higher level of service by revolutionizing the logistics. The home appliances manufacturer Dyson took an existing business and did it better through technological innovation and design. Different categories of opportunity involve different levels of risk. Introducing a new product through a new business into a new market tends to involve a higher level of risk than improving an existing service or product that already has a strong customer base.

At one end of the scale there are solutions looking for a problem. For example, somebody may have come up with new miniaturized sensors. The inventor says, 'Nobody else has been able to do this.' And the investor says, 'Fine, but what is the real market opportunity? Which industry requires this level of miniaturization?' It is a technology in search of an application.

At the other end of the scale, there are problems in search of solutions. In the software area, for instance, an executive might identify the need for a better way of managing the recruitment, training and grading of staff; he or she then writes some software to take care of that. You build up a case for the new software that solves the problem and cuts costs in the human resources department, while causing the minimum of disruption to existing work practices.

Some commercial opportunities arise because the way something is done has become outdated but the market has not yet realized it. The Waterstone's bookstore chain, which Apax backed, would be an example. Tim Waterstone realized that bookshops needed to be larger, all the stock needed to be out on display instead of hidden in the back room, and the bookshop needed to stay open late at night, seven days a week. He realized that the old model had become outdated because people's living habits had changed. During the week, they do not have time to go shopping for a book. On Saturday they are doing things with their children. Sunday is now the most important day for retail. Those who created large stores capable of selling a huge amount of stock in a single day, instead of selling the same numbers each day of the week, managed to capitalize on this change in lifestyle. Hence we have huge furniture showrooms, electrical retailers and DIY megastores that are empty during the week but packed at weekends.

Another example is cinema-going, which was regarded as a declining market by the early 1980s. American Multi-Cinema (AMC) and others looked at the market carefully and came to the conclusion that the owners and operators of old-fashioned cinemas were operating an outdated business model. They were offering one or two screens when people would prefer twelve or twenty-four screens. Within a few years, the multiplex operators had revolutionized cinema-going across the world. What had been a declining market became a growing market. That was basically a question of recognizing and satisfying latent demand. The observation was that, if you supplied a different product into that marketplace – one that provided a far greater choice of films to see – sales would shoot up. We have seen the climb in admissions ever since. In Britain alone, ticket sales rose from 55 million in 1985, when the first multiplex opened, to 165 million in 2005, by which time there were 2,453 multiplex screens, accounting for 73 per cent of all cinema screens in the country.

Other types of businesses have capitalized on trends in other countries, especially the United States, which generally leads other markets. The United States is worth observing closely as an indicator of what is likely to happen next in Europe and elsewhere. For example, we have recently seen the expansion of the personal storage business in Europe. In the United States there are about 0.65 square-metres of self-storage space available per person. In Britain it is a twentieth of that, so some entrepreneurs decided that it was time to set up storage facilities in the UK. In the initial stages of the market's development in Britain, businesses are absorbing most of the storage capacity. But in the United States, where it is a more mature market, the storage business is also serving the consumer. According to the season, your hockey sticks go in and your surfboard comes out, or your bicycles go in and your skis come out.

Before you set out on an entrepreneurial venture, ask yourself, 'Which is the most promising area for me?'

The key criteria for comparison are the size of the opportunity, your personal aptitude in the chosen market, your ability to recruit suitable managerial, technical and creative talent, the attractiveness of the business model, capital intensity, and the barriers to competition that you can establish.

The first of these criteria is the size of the opportunity. As a rule, you are better off picking an opportunity with great rather than limited potential. The size and prospective growth of the market generally dictates the size of the opportunity. Hence it is almost a reflex for a professional investor, a venture capitalist, to look at the size of the market opportunity before considering other aspects of a business proposition. Is it a large market? If the answer is no, there is not much point in investigating further.

Why is size so important? It is obvious that the larger the market, the larger the opportunity and the larger the potential reward. Growth is an important aspect of size and, in most instances, the prospect of rapid and substantial growth is attractive to entrepreneurs and investors alike. The astonishing growth of Google is an example that many businesses would like to emulate. If you want to make a lot of money when you eventually sell your company or float it, then, if it is operating in a large market in which there is great room for further expansion, this will result in a higher exit value than if it is serving a small market with limited prospects for expansion. If, for example, you set up a specialist retail operation in a saturated market, you will obtain a low valuation when you sell, because there is no growth in prospect for the purchaser.

The search for growth opportunities characterized my career at Apax. Turnarounds – taking a poorly performing company and bringing it back to health – were not our business. We were fortunate to be in venture capital and private equity at a time when there were terrific growth opportunities, both in early-stage companies and in established companies that could be the object of a buy-out. We lived through a period when new markets and new products, driven by new technologies, carried young companies forward. Growth remedies the mistakes you make and gives you room to correct shortcomings. A declining market, by contrast, can turn what might in other circumstances be a minor commercial disappointment into a significant problem.

There are, nevertheless, a few mature, even declining sectors in which, the competition having become weak, the entrepreneur can derive advantages of scale without the promise of further growth. One such example was the British food-canning industry, which Hillsdown Foods consolidated very successfully.

I have met entrepreneurs in small markets who connected with their opportunity through happenstance and felt lucky. After several years, though, when they knew the market and saw the limits of its size, they began to think differently. They realized that, far from being lucky, they were boxed into a small opportunity. They had opened the door to a cupboard rather than a ballroom.

The world of entrepreneurship, which is a world of seizing opportunities, is full of situations where people have started out without much thought. Then, years later, they take stock and realize, 'For all the effort, I ought to be able to achieve more.' It is wiser to figure that out at the beginning.

You can, of course, often find a way of switching from a smaller to a larger market and achieving greater success. Doubtless, your experience in building your small business will then be of value to you. An example of successful switching was Frank Lowy, who with his partner introduced shopping centres to Australia. They became the preferred landlord for the major retail chains. When Lowy's company, Westfield, opens a shopping centre anywhere in Australia today, retailers rush to get space in that centre. Lowy eventually discovered that Australia is actually a rather small market and he therefore began to expand into the United States.

Frank Lowy is now a big success. Westfield is the world's biggest retail property group, with assets of more than $50 billion. The company is capitalized at about $19 billion, making it the eighth-largest company on the Australian stock exchange. One of its recent ventures is a property development in London, on the site of the 2012 Olympic Games.

But did Frank Lowy, when he set out, imagine that he would be setting up an international shopping-centre company? No. He started out with a single retail food outlet; from there he changed direction and moved into residential property development; from there he changed direction again and connected with the idea of shopping centres. He and his partner took ten years to find their way. His career is an example of perseverance and trial and error successfully at work. He changed direction several times before hitting upon the business opportunity that could match his talent and ambition.

There is no single route to success. But in order to have success on a large scale you need to have big ambitions and to connect with a substantial market opportunity. If you can do that at the outset, you will achieve success sooner.

Size can also be dictated by financial resources. Autonomy was one of Apax's greatest successes: when we floated the company on the London Stock Exchange in November 2000, our $750 million profit was more than 300 times our initial investment. I remember having a meeting in an Apax conference room in Portland Place, London: the entrepreneur Mike Lynch and my colleagues John McMonigall and Peter Englander and I sat around a table. Mike Lynch was a fireman's son who had become a maths don at Cambridge and was interested in mathematical methods for recognizing information patterns. He had developed a technology to identify number sequences, for example car number-plates. He was selling this technology to police forces in Britain. He had had an offer from a large technology company, Racal, to buy him out for about $4 million. After listening to him, we said: 'Your technology is groundbreaking. Don't sell out to Racal; let's build a major company together instead. We will invest $2.5 million for a stake in the company.'

John McMonigall spent time with Mike Lynch and his team in Cambridge. They told John they were trying to recognize patterns in language; as well as recognizing numbers they were trying to see if they could develop a search engine that recognized words. John returned to the office very excited: the applications for this in the Internet age would be enormous.

Mike led Autonomy into the business information market, selling to BP, McKinsey and the defence establishment in the United States. These organizations used the software to gain rapid access to information in their own databases. Mike's strategy required relatively little capital and it worked.

In contrast, similar word-search technology was exploited through a higher-investment/higher-return strategy by Google, which aimed not at the business market but at the far larger consumer market, which it could access via the Internet. The thing about Google – and the two venture firms that backed it understood this very well – was that in that type of business you cannot generate revenues until you have created a sufficiently large network. The consumer proposition is attractive, but it means nothing until you have scale. Once Google was used by millions of consumers, advertisers were plentiful and the company became profitable.

As is well known, the Google concept was developed without capital by computer-science students Sergey Brin and Larry Page in a Stanford University bedroom in 1998. It was subsequently launched with about $1 million raised from Brin's and Page's friends and connections. In 1999 it reported just $220,000 of revenues. When they were able to demonstrate the capabilities and potential of the product, they raised considerable capital for such an early-stage company, about $25 million, from two of the world's leading venture firms, Sequoia Capital and Kleiner, Perkins, Caufield & Byers. By the time Google floated on the stock exchange in 2004, with annual revenues of more than $3 billion, the company was valued at $23 billion. At the time of writing, Google's market capitalization is $160 billion. The company is not yet ten years old.

Defining correctly which market you are in, how large it is and the size of the opportunity you have identified within it: these are the first, fundamental questions about calibrating risk and return. Autonomy, in addressing the business market, took a relatively low-investment approach. Google, addressing the consumer market, took a high-investment approach. If a firm is to grow it has to find currents that carry its products far and wide. In that sense, opportunities constantly come and go and others take advantage of them if you do not.

What makes networks like Google, Amazon and eBay unique is that, once established, each enjoys a huge barrier against new entrants. That barrier to competition is the large size of their networks. If you get there first, everyone else is effectively locked out, at least until the ball bounces again.

You always have to be watchful for the next bounce of the ball. For example, search, in itself, may not turn out to be a 'sticky' application forever. Consumers may feel no loyalty to a particular search engine and it costs neither time nor effort to switch from one to another. A competitor could one day come up with applications that draw users away from Google. The next bounce of the ball could be access to specific content that will bind users to a particular search engine.

Another example of a platform business is Federal Express. Fedex had its origins in a paper written in 1965 by Yale undergraduate Fred Smith, who noted that the airfreight business in the United States suffered from poor logistics. He saw there was an opportunity to build a major new company. He launched Fedex in 1973 with 389 employees and fourteen small planes. On its first day, the company delivered just 186 packages, and it was not until the deregulation of the air cargo market in 1977 (something for which Smith, who understood his market intimately, had lobbied hard) that it really started to build its global network.

After a shaky start, Fedex was able to float on the New York Stock Exchange in 1978, and achieved compound annual growth of about 40 per cent through the 1980s. In 1983, it became the first American company to achieve sales of $1 billion within ten years of its launch without corporate acquisitions. It now has 260,000 employees, the largest cargo fleet in the world (and reputedly the second-largest air fleet of any kind) and annual sales of $32 billion. Building that platform cost a great deal of money, raised over several rounds of finance. But now that the global platform is built, the company has the huge competitive advantage of size. It has only two serious competitors, UPS and DHL. It would be difficult for a new competitor to enter that market without making a huge financial investment. Given the dominant position of the three incumbents, that would probably be a very unattractive investment proposition.

In 2000, Apax and other private-equity firms attempted a platform investment in a joint venture with Swift, the bank transfer organization. Together, we invested in a company called Bolero. Unlike Fedex, which made an offer to which customers could easily respond without having to change the way they did business, Bolero required a major adaptation on the part of its customers. It was a paperless, computerized system for international trade, going from the order placed in one of fifty countries, all the way through the purchasing, transport, financing, insurance, letters of credit and banking to eventual fulfilment and confirmation of delivery. Everything was in one place, electronically, without the need for umpteen separate pieces of paper. In this way, the typical costs per transaction could be dramatically reduced.

The only problem was that all the suppliers to a particular firm needed to use the platform for it to be effective. But the individual supplier, if he only had one client using Bolero, did not want to change. You had, therefore, to create a large platform of both supplier and client firms in order to achieve success. Networks are 'viral': once a sufficient number of companies are doing it, all the others have to do it, they cannot afford to stay out. Eventually it will happen. But how do you create this network effect from scratch? It has to be a hugely compelling proposition. Bolero, which now focuses on the banking and financial-services sectors, worked hard to achieve that but has still not entirely succeeded.

The lesson of Bolero is that it is difficult to persuade a whole chain of participants in a market to adopt a new, disruptive technology in one go. Business models that involve climbing a series of manageable steps are generally easier to implement successfully than those that involve one huge step.

New ways of doing things are constantly being established, creating opportunities for entrepreneurs in their wake. In 1981 a deal was struck between Microsoft and mainframe-computer manufacturer IBM, according to which Microsoft would supply the operating system for IBM's latest product, the personal computer (PC), which had been introduced in response to the threat from the Apple II. Crucially, the Microsoft operating system, which was marketed as MS-DOS, could be licensed to other manufacturers. Two years later, IBM agreed to carry Microsoft's Windows software, but again did not insist on exclusivity: Microsoft was free to sell its software to other computer manufacturers. If you were smart, you drew two conclusions from these developments: first, forget about trying to develop an operating systems company for PCs; second, forget about Apple becoming a leader in that market. Apple would find an application as a niche supplier to creative businesses, because the Macintosh is versatile and designers love it, but it had lost the chance to become the PC leader. That opportunity had gone when Microsoft signed with IBM.

A new opportunity opened up when IBM entered the PC market. Dell and Compaq spotted it: to produce the same machine as IBM, capable of running the same operating system and the same Microsoft software, at lower cost. Dell, Compaq and the others had better logistics than IBM, more aggressive marketing, more efficient component supply lines and, soon enough, they introduced more sophisticated products and achieved greater scale. In launching the personal computer, IBM (market capitalization at the time of writing: $141 billion) inadvertently created Microsoft (market capitalization: $292 billion) along with Dell (market capitalization: $57 billion), Compaq, which is now owned by Hewlett-Packard (market capitalization: $108 billion), and others. As a result, IBM failed to establish itself as a significant player in the PC business. It opened the door for others to walk in. IBM recently abandoned the PC market altogether, selling its PC division to a Chinese purchaser.

Until Microsoft was signed up by IBM, Apax funds were seeking to invest in companies that were planning to make better personal computers. But as soon as the deal was done between Microsoft and IBM, we realized that the market had changed. In the future, computers and computer applications would have to be compatible with the MS-DOS operating system and Windows software.

Scale is clearly an all-important consideration. Is it a large market? Is it a large product or service opportunity? Can you take full advantage of the opportunity only by setting up a substantial platform that requires great investment? Can you build your market position step by step, or do you and your prospective customers have to climb a cliff?

The second criterion after market size is your particular aptitude and depth of understanding of your market. Do not enter a market unless you understand it as well as anyone else.

A good example of deep sector expertise is Tim Waterstone, whom I mentioned earlier. He had worked for the giant newsagent, stationer and book retailer, WH Smith. He went to open their operation in the United States and was fired. He returned to Britain and said that he believed that British bookshops were completely outdated.

He wanted to break the Net Book Agreement that maintained a cosy price-fixing relationship between publishers and bookstores at the expense of the consumer. He wanted to have shops that instead of being 1,000 square feet were going to be 10,000 or 15,000 square feet.

Apax funds invested in Tim's company when he had only a handful of shops. The whole book trade said, 'This is going to fail. It's not going to work. Publishers will not work with them. Wholesalers and small retailers will not like it.' But Tim was right. He realized that in order to be successful he needed sufficient capital to get such a volume of book purchases that the publishers could not ignore him. He worked out that he needed to get to twenty or thirty shops. If he did not get to that number it was not going to work. So he went out and raised the capital to get to the required number of shops in a short space of time. His knowledge of the market dictated his strategy.

Professor Michael Porter has observed that in every industry there is an equilibrium between suppliers, customers, competition, new technologies and the other forces influencing the market. You had better understand where those forces are concentrated, where the leverage is, if you are going to do something to change the industry. Tim Waterstone understood the industry inside out. He knew that the book publishers did not especially care about the retail trade, they cared about selling more books, and if he could manage to get himself into the position of being a major customer, then, with his new style of shop, he would outperform the existing book retailers. Who was going to go to the small shops when Waterstone's had better stock, more convenient opening hours, more competitive prices and well-informed graduate assistants? And he was very successful.

When, however, Tim tried to step outside his area of real

expertise – for example, by opening a chain of toy stores – he was less successful. The rule is simple: become expert in your field, know your market inside out.

The ultimate aim is to become the category killer in the largest market you can find. The category killer is the company that seizes the bulk of the market and makes it difficult for others to enter. Those coming behind have to fill niches.

Once Waterstone's had done it in Britain, everybody wanted to do it. After Waterstone's, there came Ottakars, Borders, Bookends and others. But none could catch the market leader.

Knowing your market means, among other things, that you launch your product to hit the market at the right time. This is crucial. When I wanted to launch venture-capital funds too early I was not able to. When the moment came, I saw the opportunities for early-stage funds, then buy-out funds, balanced funds (investing from early stage to buy-outs in Apax's chosen growth sectors) and global funds, and I adjusted or redefined the strategy of Apax accordingly each time, ahead of the anticipated bounce of the ball.

Markets are often fast moving. They also go through cycles. Clothes and food retailer Marks and Spencer has recently emerged from a bad patch. Some manufacturing companies turn to retail, like Nike and the Body Shop, which could not get shelf space in the major retail outlets and opened their own stores to sell their products. Often such a move by a successful company will change the competitive balance in the market.

The key factor in these examples is the depth of understanding of the marketplace demonstrated by the companies concerned. The more you know, the more you will be able to cope with challenges and take advantage of opportunities, and the more successful you are likely to be relative to your competition.

By contrast, gifted nephews of mine wanted to get into property in Australia. They were new to the property market. They thought: 'Why not do a residential development in Sydney?' They did not think of analysing carefully the residential property cycle. As it turned out, the cycle was turning down and they found it very difficult to sell the apartments they had developed. They just managed to get out at cost after three years of hard work. By then they had realized that becoming a residential property developer was not the most appropriate objective for them because, although it is a huge market, it is also a highly developed market; there was no worthwhile opportunity for them as a new entrant.

My nephews did some basic analysis, by speaking to the leading estate agents and others, and alighted on the idea of a specialist shopping centre in the medical field, where traffic would be driven by a group of doctors who would operate from purpose-built, modern premises, with allied services necessary for top-quality treatment. That is clearly a much smaller market than the residential market, but it is a growth niche in which they have become expert, and where there is no existing property development leader. The immaturity of the specialist-centre model means that there will be inefficiency in the market as well as high growth, which will provide them with the opportunity to be market leader.

An efficient market is a market where opportunities are priced competitively. An inefficient market is one where, because of greater uncertainty, the equilibrium between supply and demand is not efficiently reached. This provides the opportunity to make unusual profits. As a venture capitalist, you are always looking for inefficient markets because that is where unusually high returns can be achieved.

Clear examples of this are to be found in the differences between geographic markets. As the supply of venture capital and private equity increased faster in the United States than in Europe in the 1990s, returns on buy-outs were higher in Europe. Within Europe, each new market in turn – Britain, France, Germany, Spain, Italy, Israel – offered a higher return than its maturing predecessors. Today, China and India, South Korea and other south-east Asian countries, as well as Russia and Central European countries, offer higher return prospects than do the more developed Western markets.

The third criterion, after size and aptitude, is your personal ability to recruit talent in the field. Do you have, or will you be able to hire, the calibre of executives and specialist staff needed to build an outstanding business?

Talent means sector expertise, technical and creative skills. It also means being surrounded by outstanding individuals in all the generic aspects of the operations of your business. Your heads of finance and administration, sales and marketing, production management and distribution: these have to be the best people in your industry.

An entrepreneur who thinks he can do everything is fooling himself or herself. He or she will be constrained to run a small business. A successful entrepreneur who has built a large business will always be surrounded by outstanding executives who are themselves able to operate in an entrepreneurial way: they take initiative, make decisions and provide effective leadership for the people who report to them.

If you have identified a large opportunity in a large market, you have passed square one. But if you have no idea how to recruit the people needed to exploit that opportunity, or if you are not the kind of person for whom such people are likely to work, you will find it difficult to be successful.

The fourth criterion concerns the business model. By this I mean the elements of the business that drive its growth and its profitability, and the manner in which they fit together. A good business model provides significant financial rewards if the operations of the company are reasonably successful. A poor business model provides scant rewards even if the operations of the company are outstandingly successful. A leading football club can win the league title and still lose money. Why? Because, with very few exceptions, football clubs do not operate good business models.

If you operate the wrong model you will not make much money, you will find it difficult to raise capital and you will not recruit outstanding people. Investors are attracted to great business models. Talented people are attracted to great business models. The really outstanding people ask you about your business when they come for interview. They investigate your business model. They do not want to put their effort into a business that will not deliver attractive rewards.

Fundamentally, how attractive a business is it? How fast will it grow? How reliable are its projected revenue streams? How controllable are its costs? How protected are its operating margins?

Once established, will the business enjoy barriers that protect its sales and profits from competition for long?

Can growth be achieved without recourse to significant additional capital? If not, are the rewards of further investment likely to be commensurate with the risks? These are fundamental questions about the nature of your business; the more trouble you take over the answers, the better.

**Great effort
will bring
small reward
if you don't have
the right
business model**

When I got married, my wife, Sharon Harel, an entrepreneurial and creative film producer, wanted to continue to be involved in the film industry. But we intended to raise a family and the prospect of spending months filming on location did not have great appeal. Sharon had already become acutely aware of the shortcomings of independent film production, which is a very risky business requiring huge effort to raise fresh capital for each new film. So she opted instead to set up a sales and finance company whose business model involved financing films on the back of the sale of their international distribution rights. That led to the formation of Capitol Films, a successful company from which Sharon sold out last year after nearly twenty years and more than a hundred movies, among them Robert Altman's *Gosford Park* and Roman Polanski's *Death and the Maiden*.

Sharon's experience shows the importance of the business model. A model that requires the raising of production finance for each project, and in each case running a risk of great profit or great loss, is less attractive than a model based on acquiring and pre-selling international rights.

The fifth criterion is capital intensity. Can you raise the necessary capital? Different businesses require different levels of finance.

It was once possible to enter the private-equity business without much capital, assemble a small team and raise a fund. I had zero capital.

You can still enter the consulting business with little capital. There are many service businesses where the capital investment is not great. Advertising is one. The Internet is also now enabling retail and other businesses to operate with less capital than was the case in the past, because the upfront investment in an Internet-based business is often less than bricks and mortar in city centres.

On the other hand, if you wanted to create an insurance company

"IT IS NOT PRETEND, BUT IT IS
JUST LIKE A FAIRY TALE."

Few early-stage companies perform according to their business-plan forecasts – a truth that this 1996 Apax Christmas card took to its logical conclusion.

or a sophisticated manufacturing business, you would need substantial capital. Such businesses face an obvious funding challenge in the start-up phase. You have to pick an industry where the required finance can realistically be raised by you.

A business that has a low capital requirement is often a business with low barriers to entry, which is the sixth, and final, criterion to be considered. As easy as it is for you to enter a low capital sector, it is just as easy for your competitors. A business with a high capital requirement benefits from a higher barrier to entry: once you are established, you are protected from new competitors. For this reason, when you are considering the capital requirement you must consider not only the ease or difficulty of raising the money but also the subsequent competitive advantages or disadvantages that might be involved.

Having analysed two or more business opportunities, how do you make the decision about which one to pursue?

I find the decision tree very helpful. It is one of the most useful tools that I took from Harvard Business School. Essentially, it is a method for analysing the relative merits of alternative paths. The tree starts with the initial choice between one course of action and its opposite. Each course of action forms a branch, which splits between one possible outcome and another. These outcomes form further branches, which again split into possible outcomes.

I used the decision tree in 1975 when two of my original three partners left MMG and I had to decide on the way forward. Would I seek employment? Would I pursue the venture-capital opportunity? Should I reduce my vision of MMG to that of a UK-based advisory firm?

The tree started out looking something like this:

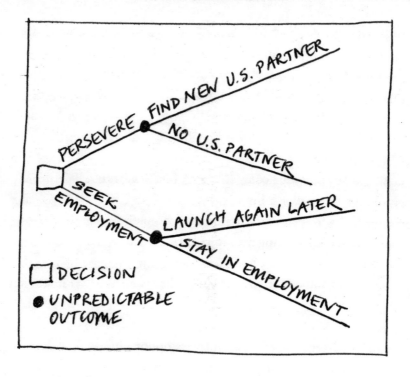

As I considered each outcome, I added more branches. The process continued until I was satisfied that I had considered every eventuality. Normally, one then applies a probability factor to each branch. In this case, for example, if I persevered how likely was it that I would find a new American partner? Or, if I went back into employment, how likely was it that I would launch again later? The combination of outcomes and probabilities gives one a robust analytical method for weighing up the initial choice.

In normal business practice, the choices mostly concern investments, and the outcomes can be expressed in numbers, whether of costs or of revenues. One can therefore go further and multiply the outcomes by the probabilities to arrive at a mathematically weighted judgement of which initial route to take.

You could apply the decision tree to your own decision to take the entrepreneurial road, as I did. Or, as I would recommend, you could use the decision tree to choose between different opportunities.

The decision tree has a further use as a means of demonstrating to colleagues how one has arrived at a particular decision. I have often found it extremely useful in this regard: the tree lays out my analytical path and enables my colleagues to follow my logic and to support or correct my analysis quickly.

Most decisions involve a trade-off: you give up something of value in return for something else. Getting these trade-offs right is what calibration is about. I have found the decision tree very helpful for this purpose also. There are plenty of useful guides on the use of decision trees to be found on the Internet, not least on the Harvard Business School website.

There are two further considerations that impact on your choice of opportunity: the degree to which you will be in control of the key elements of the business, and the prospect of extraordinary gain, known as uncapped potential.

As a private-equity firm, one of the criteria that Apax strayed from at its peril was that of ensuring that we were in control of the key elements of the companies we backed. The heaviest loss Apax suffered was in our German operation, in the privatization of Bundesdruckerei, which printed banknotes for the German Federal Government and produced telephone smart cards for Deutsche Telekom.

No sooner had we invested in the business than the German telecommunications sector got into difficulties and sales of smart cards were badly hit. We tried to downsize the business and were prepared to invest more capital, but, in the interlocking worlds of German business, government and trade unions, we were not able to get agreement on the lay-offs. We ended up taking a €140 million (then about $140 million) loss and handing over our shares to the banks. We decided not to pour good money after bad. Stakeholders other than the shareholders controlled Bundesdruckerei's destiny.

After this experience, we were never again tempted by situations in which the venture was dependent upon or strongly influenced by political considerations. We later turned down investments because they depended on government regulation or subsidies. Politics and business follow different agendas.

Bundesdruckerei taught me another lesson. When the economic situation worsens, the position of lending banks is crucial. If their loans are fully secured (usually against the assets and/or shares of the company), they will seize that security to recover their money, often driving the business into liquidation in the process. If they are insufficiently covered, they will be more inclined to support the company through to recovery. The lesson is to make sure you have a management team the banks trust and, if you get into trouble, make changes to the team before the bank forces those changes upon you.

An overarching factor in choosing the right opportunity is what venture capitalists call uncapped potential. At Apax, we learned to search for situations that offered a blue-sky scenario, a chance to get lucky. Sometimes these scenarios do materialize. One example was our investment in Azimut, an investment management company that we purchased from BPE, an Italian bank that found itself forced to divest Azimut because of the financial pressures bearing down upon it.

The transaction was fairly valued. The investment management business in Italy was undeveloped. Azimut was led by an excellent team. It had a strong position in the market and was likely to prove a sound investment. As it turned out, the stock exchange cycle went in our favour. What had been a good investment became a great investment. We floated the company on the Milan stock exchange in 2004, with an IPO value of $725 million. We sold the final tranche of our shares in June 2005. We made more than three times our money in two years.

Sometimes a new factor will emerge suddenly that throws into question the whole calibration of an opportunity. One such event occurred in the negotiation to acquire Bezeq, the Israeli national telecommunications provider, in which we partnered with Haim Saban's Saban Capital Group and Arkin Communications. Haim Saban and I are twins of a kind. We are the same age, we both left Egypt in 1957, we both spent time in Israel and we both found ourselves looking at Bezeq, which the Israeli government decided to privatize in 2005.

We closed the transaction, in my Tel Aviv apartment, after an exhausting negotiation and a complex tender process with hugely complicated rules; there had been three groups bidding, one dropped out and the other offered less than we did. We finally agreed to buy the Israeli government's 30 per cent stake for $1 billion, with an option to buy a further 10.7 per cent. The investment made our joint-venture group the largest shareholder in Bezeq.

Almost immediately, news came that Bezeq's management had been interviewed by the police. It was alleged that the company had used private intelligence-gathering specialists to collect information about the market position of its competitors. These specialists were being investigated, it was said, for using Trojan Horse software that burrows its way into the computer systems of the target, which in this case would have been Bezeq's competitors, and comes back with secret information. This is a criminal offence. All of a sudden there was a potential lawsuit against Bezeq. Our hearts sank.

This development presented several potential risks for the investment. First, if the allegations were true, we would be associated with wrongdoing and our reputation would be damaged. Second, Bezeq's management could be jailed, which would imperil implementation of our plans for improving the company's operations and profitability. Third, a lawsuit, whatever the outcome, could prove to be a costly distraction for Bezeq's management over a long period of time, and the company could incur substantial legal costs. Fourth, Bezeq might suffer significant damages if a lawsuit went against it.

A meeting with many participants was held, including Bezeq's management, our legal advisers and a gifted and prominent litigation lawyer and great friend of mine, Dori Klagsbald, as well as the Apax and Saban teams. The deal was in the balance at the start of the meeting. Someone said, 'We are not going to invest, it's too large a risk.' But Dori Klagsbald counselled that it might not turn out to be such a serious problem. In the end, we concluded that the damage to the company and the danger to our reputation could be contained. We obtained some compensation from the Israeli government to cover our legal exposure and potential expenses, and the deal closed in October 2005. In the event, the Trojan Horse issue fell away.

In summary, picking the right opportunity always involves a feeling of uncertainty. You have to be convinced that the opportunity matches your skills and that it is likely to offer an attractive business model that can deliver the growth and profitability necessary to make your vision a reality.

The hardest calibration arises in situations of adversity, such as occurred when my MMG partners quit in 1975. Although the conditions that prevailed in the early 1970s were not conducive to the development of venture capital in the short term, I had gained a strong sense in the United States that there was going to be a powerful drive to support smaller businesses. I was there when the ferment about growth companies led to the formation of the venture-capital industry. I was sure it would happen in Europe. I had a conviction that this would be a huge opportunity, and that the first mover would have a great advantage. I crossed off the other branches of the decision tree and was more determined than ever to pursue the venture-capital opportunity.

In taking the road to private equity, even in the early 1970s and despite the scepticism of my departing partners, I made the right decision. It did turn out to be a huge opportunity. All I needed to be successful was to stick with it.

4

TIMING IS EVERYTHING

A second bounce
usually follows
a change in the trend
or in the cycle.

When I was at Oxford I heard the story of a don who used to drink heavily at High Table. Outside the dining hall in the middle of the quad was a solitary tree. One night the don strayed from the path after dinner, bumped into the solitary tree, fell down and got up and bumped into it again. An undergraduate rushed to help him as he was getting up for the third or fourth time, only to hear him say, 'Losht, losht in a bloody foresht!'

Many entrepreneurs do not really see the context in which they are operating. They are lost in what they think is a forest. Entrepreneurs need to know where they are in relation to trends and cycles. They also have to be sure not to confuse one with the other.

Market trends and cycles are what entrepreneurial timing is primarily about. They are the areas on which you must focus to reduce market uncertainty. Unfortunately, many entrepreneurs operate completely oblivious to these considerations.

It was our first chairman, Maurice Schlogel, who used to encourage us to anticipate 'the second bounce of the ball', as he called it. Where and when will it bounce next? If you really understand your market you will get to the correct answer. You will be able to take advantage of the next bounce of the ball, the one that is hard to judge.

In the private-equity industry the first bounce of the ball in the United States and, later, in Europe was venture capital, backing start-up or early-stage companies. The second bounce of the ball was buy-outs, where private-equity firms purchased established, generally private companies that were not achieving their full potential. The next bounce of the ball was funds that could be invested in a number of countries, not just one. If you saw these bounces ahead of time you could be ahead of your competitors. If you opened offices internationally in 1988 or 1990, as we did at Apax, instead of waiting until the multi-country bounce took place in 2000, you would have gained an advantage and raised and invested larger funds than strictly national competitors. Many private-equity firms have opened offices in recent years in Europe as well as the United States, and some have opened in Japan.

The current bounce of the ball is the global one: funds that are not limited to particular territories but can be invested anywhere – in the United States, Europe, Japan, India, China or the rest of Asia. As a result, private-equity firms are now busy opening offices in India and China.

We have seen a sequence of bounces in all industries. A bounce often follows a change in the trend or a turn in the cycle. In the computer industry, for example, at the time when the switch from mainframe to personal computers was about to occur, some thought that the second bounce of the ball would be that businesses as well as consumers would purchase PCs from retail outlets. Specialist retail ventures were duly launched.

Apax funds made an early-stage investment in a company called Computacenter, which thought differently. The insight that Computacenter had was that if businesses were going to buy a large number of computers they were not going to do it by queuing in line at a retail store. They were going to need – and they would expect – a sophisticated supplier. Since you cannot sell hardware without selling software at the same time, you are going to have to go into the problem-solving, software business also. Computacenter, which correctly anticipated the second bounce from mainframes to PCs in the business world, went to major firms that had a significant demand for computer power and tailored software – such as insurance companies – and said, 'You are spending so much on your mainframes, we can shift you to PCs and you will be able to do all these things much more cheaply than you can today.'

Computacenter invested in a sophisticated, IBM-style sales force to address business clients. It became a trusted supplier in a new field because it anticipated the second bounce correctly and invested to take advantage of it.

Later on, as the market developed, Computacenter realized that there was a further opportunity in the marketplace: to buy back all the computers they had installed in their clients' operations – because their clients were struggling to manage their PC networks – and to run them on the clients' behalf. They said: 'We are not going to sell you a computer, we are going to provide a complete computer solution: hardware, software, maintenance, upgrades, the works.' Instead of companies buying their own computers and having their own IT people, Computacenter offered: 'We'll take all this burden off your back.'

This is an example of anticipating the bounces of the ball in the market trend. If Computacenter had not taken advantage of these opportunities, somebody else would have. Had they stood still, Computacenter would have found their market-share shrinking, not growing. Computacenter floated on the London Stock Exchange in 1998, achieving an IPO value of just over $2 billion. It was a successful investment for us; we made more than $500 million.

Another early-stage investment where we anticipated the bounce in the trend was Q-Cell, an alternative energy company and the world's second-largest manufacturer of electricity-generating solar cells. We saw ahead of time that alternative energy would become attractive, and we looked for companies active in that market which had products coming on stream that might make them candidates for flotation. Apax funds invested about $11 million in Q-Cell and made about $309 million profit in three years, after the company went public on the Deutsche Börse.

The Q-Cell story was all about seeing a new sector, a new opportunity ahead of others. Alternative energy was on the way to becoming a hot sector, and we knew we would do well if we could identify a company with a decent product offering. The Q-Cell investment was really a pre-initial public offering, or pre-flotation, round of finance. In other words, we had the IPO in view at the very beginning. And when the public markets understood the importance of alternative energy and offered us an attractive price, we sold out.

The tide raises all boats. Q-Cell benefited from the fact that the valuations of all energy companies were going up, and those of alternative energy companies were going up even higher.

Of course there is a danger that if you launch your product too early you will struggle; you might even fail, even if you get the market's direction right. This is especially true of capital-intensive ventures. The Swatch car might be an example, or hybrid engines. It is advantageous to enter the market early and to be well positioned when it takes off, but the danger if you are there too early is that you run out of capital before the market develops and you are its leader.

You could argue that I started in private equity in Europe eight years too soon. You could argue that Apax went into Germany ten years too soon. But the private-equity business is not capital intensive – it does not cost very much to be open for business – and there is a huge strategic advantage in being first. You accumulate experience of the market, you build up networks of contacts who refer investments to you, you build a brand, and you understand the market better than later entrants. If you tried to build a major private-equity firm from scratch today it would be difficult. If you tried to get into the hedge-fund business today it would be tougher than it was seven or eight years ago.

One of the decisions that may have gone the wrong way at Apax was the decision not to get into the hedge-fund business in 2000. The emergence of hedge funds marked the beginning of a market trend. The hedge funds' use of derivatives, for instance, had the potential to transform investment management. I believed we should be part of that trend. I proposed entering the hedge fund business, but most of my partners were against.

I had agreed with my partners that I would leave the firm on my sixtieth birthday in 2005. It would certainly have made the succession more difficult if my partners were also having to cope with a complex new business. My colleagues opted for focus; I did not argue hard with them.

*

99

There are all kinds of investment funds in the market. There are venture-capital funds exclusively devoted to investing in start-ups and early-stage ventures. There are private-equity funds, such as the funds raised by Apax in my time, which can invest in early-stage ventures and/or buy-outs. There are mutual funds in which members of the public can buy shares, which invest in everything from new ventures to publicly traded stocks.

Pension funds, insurance companies, trusts, university endowment funds, charitable foundations and various national investment companies invest in all of these. Taken together, these are what we call the institutional investors who provide capital to the markets.

Then there are individual investors who buy shares in companies and funds alongside these institutional investors.

In 2000, hedge funds were not new, but they were entering a period of phenomenal growth that would see them overtake the private-equity industry in terms of capital under management. They are mostly not open to the general public: the money is raised mainly from sophisticated, high-net-worth individuals and from institutional investors. In this respect, hedge funds are the same as private-equity funds and, like private equity, they are subject to light-touch regulatory oversight. (Mutual funds and other funds sold to the general public are heavily regulated to protect the investor.) And again like private equity, the hedge-fund managers take a management fee and a share of the gain.

Unlike private-equity funds, hedge funds are not limited to investing in private companies. In fact, they invest in anything that takes their fancy: private companies, publicly traded stocks, debt, bonds, derivatives – whatever they think can provide a gain. Hedge funds often follow complex investment strategies, for example hedging the risks of one investment against another. This provides protection against high volatility of market or company performance.

Hedge-fund managers take their share of profits each year; in private equity, we take our share when we turn the investments into cash, and very often, as was the case with Apax funds, only when we have repaid all the initial capital of the fund.

Unlike private equity, most hedge funds tend to be in and out of investments quite quickly. They are opportunistic; they are not generally in the business of adding value. By the same token, their investors can generally redeem their holdings in the funds at relatively short notice, whereas in private equity investors are locked in for the term of the fund, which is usually ten years. As a result, hedge funds are more liquid, meaning that their holdings can be easily converted to cash, than private-equity funds, which are very illiquid.

I believed that hedge funds were a natural extension of the private-equity business. I thought that Apax should have hedge funds, both because I believed in the hedge-fund model and because I thought that having investment skills in public stocks as well as private companies made good sense.

If you look at the leaders in the private-equity business today, many – Apollo, Bain, Blackstone and Carlyle – have launched hedge funds.

They saw the next bounce of the ball, in this case not a turn in the cycle but a change in the trend, which was for the leaders of the private-equity industry to expand beyond private equity into management of alternative assets. 'Alternative asset' today means any difficult class of investment where you can achieve inordinately high returns. Venture capital and private equity would be included and at various times, depending on the markets, the term might embrace certain aspects of public stocks, currencies, property and commodities. It also includes swaps, derivatives and other complex instruments, the use of which requires talented, highly remunerated people.

There was no bad feeling about the decision not to go into hedge funds. We considered it fully and at the right time. My colleagues took a more conservative approach than I did, and they may yet derive full advantage from being a pure private-equity firm. The important point is to be sensitive to any potential change in the trend in your market, and to consider whether and how to take advantage of it.

In the early 1980s, Apax funds invested in Sir Clive Sinclair's business, Sinclair Research, principally because we believed that Clive, a talented hi-tech innovator, could anticipate the bounces of the consumer electronics ball as well as anyone. Clive introduced the world's first laptop computer and the first genuinely portable television. He had clear visions of the future: cheap cellular phones to which you could download all kinds of media; telephones and computers in one device; a personal communications number that you could use anywhere in the world; television, music, data, books, office records, all on a single, portable machine. Each one of these predictions has come to pass, and each has created opportunities for both existing and new companies. Companies operating in the consumer electronics area have come to realize that, if they do not catch the next bounce of the ball in industries that are changing fast, they will soon be out of business.

If you achieve sufficient scale in cellular phones you can be a leader, like Nokia. Otherwise, you run the risk of being eliminated, as Ericsson was: forced to sell its cellular operations to a joint venture with Sony. Nokia reached its present position by shifting out of the manufacture of rubber boots and into new areas of technology. A smokestack-industry leader transformed itself into a technology leader. Nokia now has the challenge of predicting the next bounce of that particular ball. They might ask: 'Is this the right time to redefine our market away from the cellular business into a different business?'

In the case of Apple, it took a long time to shift from proprietary, Motorola-manufactured microprocessors, which rendered its computers incompatible with the industry-standard PCs, to using the same Intel processors as the IBM clones. For many years, Apple, protective of the uniqueness of its products, resisted this change. But Apple's chief executive officer (CEO), Steve Jobs, saw that the next bounce of the ball would be to extend Apple technology into music, books and video, and he realized that consumers would be wary of these new products if they were incompatible with Windows software.

In fact, while shifting to Intel processors, Jobs built a new operating system, OSX, which is fully compatible with Windows, thereby eliminating any fear of incompatibility for a new product, the iPod, which anticipated a bounce in the market for music that few saw coming.

When it introduced the iPod, Apple somersaulted over Sony, which had the Walkman. Sony now has an equivalent MP3 device but it is playing catch-up. iPod is the category killer.

Sony has since introduced the electronic book and Apple has launched the iPhone, a 'smart' phone that combines voice, e-mail, web-browsing and music. It has also introduced the Apple TV, which combines the interactive communications, entertainment and information functions of the television and personal computer.

Apple is no longer a computer company (in fact, the company is

"BLACKBERRY, RASPBERRY... ME YOU WON'T EVEN HAVE TO HOLD!"

After the hi-tech bubble burst in 2000, despondency about hi-tech followed. We wanted to remind everyone of the incessant drive of technological innovation, hence this 2003 Christmas card cartoon.

no longer called Apple Computer), it is a consumer electronics company, competing with Sony, Philips and Toshiba.

For its part, Sony did something extraordinary when, in 1995, it introduced the PlayStation. At that time, the games industry was moving from console games to games that could be played on personal computers. Sony seemingly went against the trend by launching the most sophisticated console to date. The PlayStation was a stunning success and launched a new trend of high-capacity consoles.

There are, inevitably, plenty of examples of new products being introduced at the wrong time, of trying to anticipate change and getting it wrong. In Britain, in May 1992, after many years of consumer research, Hutchison, a Hong-Kong-based tele-communications company, introduced Rabbit, a one-way mobile-phone service that could not receive calls and only worked close to land stations. These were usually located in shops or post offices and could be identified by a large Rabbit sign above the door. A few months later, genuine, two-way mobile services flooded the market and Rabbit disappeared into a hole. Operations ceased in December 1993, a mere twenty months after the launch, by which time Hutchison had reportedly spent between $200 million and $500 million and had a grand total of 2,000 customers.

Undaunted, Hutchison were to be major investors in Orange, an all-digital mobile network that was introduced in Britain in April 1994; they took advantage of that particular bounce of the ball with considerable success.

Another example of wrong timing was Silver Screen, a start-up DVD retail business in which Apax funds lost many millions. The idea was to set up DVD stores that would be the equivalent of Waterstone's in terms of depth of choice, opening hours and attractive retail environment. But selling films in the form of DVDs in retail stores proved to be a tough proposition. We got it wrong. We thought that High Street DVDs would fight against Internet sales and video-on-demand much more effectively than proved to be the case. Despite the fact that Silver Screen had a sophisticated management team, which produced an apparently robust business plan, they could not maintain the level of sales that was required for the business to survive.

Now that new DVD-burning technology is being introduced, and retail outlets will be able to sell from a huge back-catalogue by pressing DVDs on the spot, the retail concept may well be tackled again with better success.

Two points arise from this. The first is that, as an entrepreneur, you are always trying to take advantage of uncertainty; that entails the risk of things not turning out as you expect. The second is that what is a good idea at the planning stage can turn out to be not such a good idea when you actually get into the market. We would have been better off waiting for more information about online film purchases to be surer about the direction of the retail DVD market.

Another Apax investment where the timing was wrong was James Neill, which manufactures hand tools under the James Neill brand and garden tools under the Spear & Jackson brand. Neill was a British public company; when we bought it we were in a bidding contest with Sandvik, the Scandinavian tool manufacturer. We won the bid, but it turned out to be a hard, ten-year slog to get our money back.

The acquisition was made in 1989. We borrowed a significant sum of money. No sooner had we bought the company than the floor fell out of the British economy, bringing down the tool business with it. Engineering output in Britain fell in 1990 and 1991. Hacksaw-blade sales, which were the mainstay of the company's profits, fell with it.

All of a sudden, the business was into serious loss. We were unable to service the debt. I had to renegotiate with the lending banks, and I had to approach our fund's investors to inject more money, since our investment in Neill had reached the maximum percentage of the fund allowed by our investor agreements. It was a hot and heavy discussion. Many of our fund's investors feared that we had made a bad investment and they did not want to throw good money after bad. In the end, fortunately, they backed our judgement.

Then we found a way to get lucky. One of the lenders to James Neill, Westinghouse Finance, got into trouble. We managed to buy the Westinghouse loans at a 90 per cent discount. This enabled us to wipe out more than $30 million of James Neill's debt; we were then back in a position to save our investment.

We had to put in as managing director one of the Apax partners, Jeffrey Wilkinson, who had been joint CEO of industrial control systems and switching business Lucas Industries, to lead the company to recovery.

Although the company had two 100-year-old premium brands – James Neill and Spear & Jackson – it had been poorly managed for many years. We had analysed the market sector in great detail before making the acquisition but we, and the consultants advising us, underestimated the speed with which the sector would come under attack from Chinese imports.

Jeffrey Wilkinson, a superb manager, closed down some of the unprofitable product lines, launched others, outsourced some of the production, rebranded, closed factories and turned the company around. Eventually we did an innovative deal to get our investment back. We found US Industries (USI), which owned Ames Tools in the United States.

USI was interested in acquiring James Neill. But they were not

"THIS IS THE SHAREHOLDER HUG.
THE BANKING HUG IS NEXT DOOR..."

By 1993, many buy-outs backed by syndicates of private-equity firms and the banks that had financed them were deeply in trouble. Our Christmas card that year managed to make light of the situation.

prepared to pay the price we wanted. They expected to improve the profitability of the firm over three years. So we said, 'Fine, you will pay us the full price three years from now when you have brought about these improvements.'

That was a gutsy deal to do. We took a risk and, in fact, within three weeks of the final payment, USI's share price, for entirely unconnected reasons, dropped dramatically. If we had missed the final payment by three weeks, the story might have had a different ending.

As it was, we got 100 per cent of our money back. But, from acquisition to disposal, it took ten years of hard work.

That we persevered was crucial in terms of the culture of Apax, as well as our reputation with our investors. It became known that when an Apax investment got into trouble, we had the determination and management skills to pull ourselves out of it.

Most people would have given up with James Neill. Even some at Apax argued that we should write off the investment and focus on new, profitable opportunities. But it was important for me that on a large acquisition like that – one of our earliest buy-outs – we should show that we were capable of retrieving the situation. Nor did I want the banks that had backed us, and then supported us through the turn-around, to lose money. In the event, the banks got much more than their capital back.

James Neill illustrates two aspects of timing. One has to do with understanding your marketplace and anticipating any change in the underlying trend. The second concerns the economic cycle.

Cycles were a constant subject of discussion at Apax. We would ask: 'Is this the time to get into retailing given the consumer cycle? Is this the point to invest in technology, given the IPO cycle? Is this the time to invest in manufacturing in this sector given the investment cycle? Should we be investing in Germany given that the economic cycle in Germany is at a low?' Cycles are just as important in getting ahead as trends.

For Apax as a private-equity firm, this was a matter of when to get into and when to get out of an investment; when to get into and out of different sectors, such as telecommunications, healthcare, financial services and energy, and different types of investment opportunity, such as early-stage, growth, buy-outs and privatizations.

Sometimes you have to sit out the cycle, you have to hold on to your investment as it goes through highs and lows. We bought James Neill, demand collapsed, we held on to the company until demand came back up again.

In the mid-1980s, there was so much venture capital around and prices were so high for early-stage companies that we stayed out of the market for six or seven months and did not invest. Prices were too high.

If you work on an international scale you are sometimes able to identify different cycles between geographic markets. Certain sectors are more highly valued in one market than in another. This provides opportunity. When we bought Kabel Deutschland, the largest television station in Germany, from Deutsche Telekom, we knew we were buying at a cheap price, at a low point in the German cable-industry cycle.

The cost per viewer of purchasing a cable station in the United States and elsewhere in the world was higher than it was in Germany at that time. Deutsche Telekom had fallen into difficulties, needed to sell assets to raise cash, and was prepared to accept whatever price it could get in the market. The timing issue was a matter of recognizing the low valuations at the time we were buying, and what valuations might be achieved by the time we were ready to sell. We held the investment for about three years. Valuations of European cable companies rose, as we expected, and management succeeded in increasing the profits of the company. When we sold our stake to Providence Equity Partners in February 2006, we made about three times our money on a $220 million investment.

You have to accommodate markets. There are seasons for buying and seasons for selling. When Deutsche Telekom was in trouble and looking to sell, we bought. When everybody wanted to buy cable-company shares, we sold.

If valuations are low and people are looking to sell, that is generally a good time to buy. If valuations are going up and people are looking to buy, that is generally a good time to sell. In 2000, at the peak of the hi-tech bubble, prices of technology stocks were so high they were bound to come down; the valuations of young tech companies could not be justified. Selling became not only desirable but essential.

I remember, towards the end of the hi-tech frenzy, when the market had reached dizzying heights, an annual Apax strategy meeting at which a young, highly intelligent, normally low-key associate made an impassioned plea for us to reduce the level of our due diligence. The flow of opportunities was such, he said, that our competitors were seizing opportunities right and left and, if we insisted on maintaining rigorous standards of due diligence, we were going to miss out.

It looked to him as if we were failing to shoot fish in a barrel fast enough. He pleaded that we should give members of our team the ability to make decisions on investments if they were able to get just one director to agree.

I told him to forget it: 'You are reading this all wrong. This is a feeding frenzy and people are throwing discrimination out of the window and pushing money out, driven by fear, ego and greed, but they do not realize what they are doing. The last thing we should do is let go of our investment discipline.'

Shortly after that meeting, I spent the millennium new year's eve in Carmel, California, with my family and my in-laws. I was telling my father-in-law, Yossi Harel, that I felt the peak of the hi-tech market had surely been reached. Being in leafy Carmel it would have been easy to loosen my grip on reality. But I could not accept the valuations that were being put on companies by an overheated market. Those valuations bore no relation to underlying financial reality. In ten years from 1991, the Nasdaq hi-tech index rose from 414 points to 5,250 points. By March 2000, share prices on Nasdaq were quoted on an average of 72-times earnings. In other words, if an average company made $10 profit per share, its shares were deemed to be worth $720. $10 profit on a $720 share is a yield of less than 1.4 per cent: new investors would have done better putting their money on deposit in a bank. Many individual stocks were on even higher multiples. It made no sense at all given the commercial prospects of many of the companies in question. Clearly, there had to be a downward adjustment of share prices. A couple of days later, I visited some leading venture-capital firms in Silicon Valley and those meetings reinforced my reading of the market.

When I returned to London we accelerated the disposal of our hi-tech stocks. As a result, when the market crashed we were relatively safe. As mentioned earlier, we made seven times our money in our £150 million 1995 fund, which held a high proportion of hi-tech companies in its portfolio. We realized about £1 billion from its investments.

Not everyone was so fortunate. Those left holding hi-tech stocks when the market crashed lost a lot of money.

*

There are businesses which are uncorrelated or even contra-cyclical to the broad economy. Film is a contra-cyclical example. When the economy contracts, people spend less on travel, holidays, theatre and eating out and more on cinema tickets and DVDs. If you invest in cinemas ahead of an economic downturn your investment could benefit from the cycle. Health-related businesses and retirement homes are generally uncorrelated.

A year ago, I asked a famed investment manager what was going to happen in the financial markets and he said, 'World interest rates are too low, they have to go up.' People had been saying that year after year but it had not happened. Then, in 2006, it happened with a vengeance. We went from 1.5 per cent in the United States to 5.25 per cent in a single year. A huge jump. If you saw it coming you could profit from it or, at least, protect yourself against it. If you did not, you could miss out or suffer.

The move in interest rates did not necessarily represent a long-term trend, it represented a stage in the business cycle. You must not confuse the cycle with the trend.

What do I mean by that? When the technology bubble burst in 2000, you might have said, 'Oh, technology is dead.' But technology was not dead. Technology goes in spurts. We had a downturn in the valuations of hi-tech companies in the early 1990s; everything was overvalued from 1998 onwards; the bubble burst in 2000 and all of a sudden no one wanted to talk about technology – all in the space of a decade. But if you look at the convergence of technologies it is clear that technology will drive growth during the whole of the twenty-first century. Never confuse the technology cycle and the technology trend. The technology cycle went to a low, but in the long-term the technology trend is still pointing strongly upwards.

There will be many more tech mini-bubbles in the future: it will be like a continually refilled glass of champagne, as new technologies emerge and converge, creating new markets and new investment opportunities.

Understanding where you are in the cycle in your particular sector is crucial. If you enter a venture at the top of its market cycle, you are setting yourself a much harder task than if you go in at the bottom. At the top, prices are high, competition is fierce and profitability and values are about to decline. A combination of high rents and declining consumer spending, for example, is not a good circumstance in which to enter the retail market.

Despite this fact, business cycles are something that few young entrepreneurs think about when they launch their ventures. Why? Because they have not been there, they have not ridden cycles. They do not worry about business cycles because they know nothing about them.

I have seen the 1972–1975 recession, the 1980–1984 recession, the 1989–1993 recession, the 1995–2000 upturn and the crash of 2000–2003. I have been through cycles many times and I have seen them in many different sectors. I have become highly sensitive to cycles as a result.

Is the economy strong or weak? Is consumer spending rising or falling? Is the level of savings rising or falling? Young entrepreneurs seldom consider these crucial factors. Too often, the young entrepreneur is like a sailor leaving port without considering the weather. It is unwise.

Nobody can be 100 per cent sure about how the economy is going to behave. The greatest pundits disagree. When you draft your business plan you have to ensure that it is not totally dependent on a single economic outcome. You need a sense of what happens if, for example, interest rates go up, consumer spending declines, unemployment increases and retail sales fall.

If retail sales fall by 3 per cent, what is the impact on your profits and cash-flows? When you are in a retail business and you have invested at the top of the cycle, the impact can be very significant.

Like the sailor studying the weather charts, you have to read the financial press, brokers' reports and trade magazines, so that you understand how the broad economy and your specific sector are likely to behave. There is so much access to information now that even small businesses can know where they are in the overall economic picture.

It is possible to identify early indicators of the economic trends in each sector. Is yellow-page advertising holding firm? Are classified job ads buoyant? How buoyant is the newspaper advertising business? These are three early indicators of the future strength of the consumer economy. Similarly, construction growth and motor-vehicle order books are good indicators of future employment levels.

You must be alert to the economic environment, and use the experience you accumulate to anticipate the future better than your competitors: to see further than the headlights on the dark, winding road on which you and your competitors are travelling.

Once you know the road, then, while you are climbing and night is falling and others might be worrying about where they are going, you know there is likely to be a downhill stretch to follow and you take advantage of that knowledge. You reduce your overheads in anticipation of the downturn, or postpone a possible investment in additional capacity, because you can see further than the headlights.

Timing, trends and cycles have as big an influence on entrepreneurial success as good ideas, financial acumen and great team-building.

"WE HAVE BEEN HERE BEFORE, CARRUTHERS!"

By 2002, we had been round different economic and industry cycles so many times that each new economic development brought on a sense of déjà vu.

*

One spectacular example of deriving advantage from timing is Apax's acquisition of Mölnlycke. This deserves to be a classic business-school case study.

We wanted to buy Mölnlycke, a Scandinavian manufacturer of wound-dressings. They had fantastic technology. They made wound-dressings that were non-stick for which there was increasing international demand. But we were unable to agree on a price with Nordic Capital, the Scandinavian private-equity firm that owned the company, and we were anxious not to overpay.

Given our interest in the sector, we had also turned our attention to two humdrum wound-dressing businesses owned by a British quoted company, London Rubber Company (LRC). These were Regent Medical and Medlock Medical, both of which LRC wanted to sell at reasonable prices.

We bought them knowing that if we merged them into Mölnlycke later there would be huge synergies: profitability would immediately be lifted and the British market access of Mölnlycke would be significantly extended.

Over the course of a year or so we improved the profitability of the two companies and then used them to acquire Mölnlycke. We paid more than we had originally offered, but Mölnlycke's profits had improved in the meantime, and we had the prospect of real savings after the merger, so we were able to raise significant debt for the combined business. We acquired all three businesses with about $110 million of equity.

All this is about timing. We could not do a deal on Mölnlycke a year earlier. We had to pay more later. Meanwhile, we had made these two strategic acquisitions. We put in an experienced member of our team, Jon Samuel, as CEO of Regent and Medlock initially –

and after the acquisition as CEO of the combined group – to bring about the planned synergies and effect the merger of the companies. The strategy was a great success. We sold out to Investor AB and Morgan Stanley Principal Investors at an enterprise value of just under $3 billion. In the space of three years, we had made more than thirteen times our money, something of a record even for a growth buy-out.

The key element in this success was our understanding of growth prospects in the sector and our ability to take advantage of the synergies between these three businesses, as well as our grasp of tactical timing.

There is a negative aspect of timing that sometimes characterizes entrepreneurial endeavours: indecent haste. Indecent haste is what all too often happens to entrepreneurs when a sector gets overheated, as was the case with the hi-tech bubble of 1999–2000. Those who were impulsive suffered when the bubble burst.

Indecent haste can be a matter of doing the basic due diligence but then skipping two or three necessary steps to jump to a wished-for but unwarranted conclusion. You are really eager to complete the deal and you are impatient with the process of investigation.

Indecent haste can apply to the decision to invest, to the contract that you sign for the acquisition or with a supplier or customer you really want, or to the hiring of a star executive who might otherwise go to the competition. You get nervous. You do not want to miss the opportunity. You rush into the transaction.

Indecent haste means running the risk of overlooking something that turns out to be major. You can sign away your birthright. Let us suppose that you are moving house and you are so stressed by the process, which comes amid all kinds of other pressures to do with jobs and family, that you ignore the fact that there is a restrictive covenant on the new property, or that there is a defect in the title, or that some other party has a right of access over your land. You forge ahead with the deal just to get it done. You regret it forever after. The same happens in business.

There are plenty of examples of rushing in too fast. This does not apply only to setting up, it also applies to the way you build the company: rushing too fast and cutting corners, and in the end taking much longer to get where you want to be.

I was talking to my nephews after their hasty foray into Australian residential development. For the new move into medical shopping centres, I suggested they needed to prepare an accurate map before they could decide what to do. On this map they needed to have all the suppliers of specialist medical services in the area, all the shopping centres with parking, all doctor's surgeries, existing medical centres and so on. They should also define what the criteria would be for a successful medical centre, so that they could see which sites on the map met those criteria.

They knew they did not want their centres to be located too close to an existing competitor. They needed to work out what the revenues per specialist medical provider were likely to be in their locations, as opposed to secondary locations that were not destinations in themselves. They needed to find out, if a service provider put itself in a centre that was attracting traffic, what its revenues were likely to be compared with that provider's current locations. They needed to know what this would imply for the service provider's profitability.

In this way they could begin to understand the economics driving their prospective customers, so that when the prospective tenant says, 'I cannot afford to pay so much rent,' they can say, 'Sure you can. You are paying a certain percentage of your takings now. We are asking you to pay a lesser portion of your takings, which are likely to be higher in this centre.'

You have to understand your own business model and your clients' business models, because when an investor looks at a business plan and tries to assess how credible your sales figures are, he will call up prospective tenants and ask them how much they can afford to pay. If this property venture was looking to raise capital, prospective investors would ask: 'Why do you assume that you will manage to get this percentage of sales in rent from these tenants?' You need to be able to reply that if the average for the industry is so much, and if your centre really does act as a magnet and your tenants benefit from significantly increased footfall, they will achieve higher sales per square foot than in another location. You can ask the tenants to pay more rent because for them it is an attractive opportunity.

These calculations are about understanding more than just the marketing dimension of the business you are in. You are like the general who surveys the hills and begins to see dimensions that others do not see. Like Napoleon at the battle of the Pyramids or at Marengo: the sun is going to rise over this rather than that hill; you should attack from this direction at this time so that the enemy has the sun in their eyes. You are trying to achieve an 'unfair' advantage over competitors.

My experience has shown that you can seldom do too much due diligence. There is eventually a stage where you say, 'The only way I am going to find out is to try it on the market and see how the market reacts.' But it is most important to have a sounding board to confirm that you have reached that point, someone whose opinion you trust, because the instinct of the entrepreneur is to get going, whereas the instinct of the venture capitalist is to analyse and test until the proposition is proven, to protect the downside as well as trying to capture the upside. Having a trusted sounding board who has a dispassionate view is extremely valuable.

If you expend the effort on the wrong concept or on the wrong site, it may take you years to recover. Pitfalls should be avoided, because pitfalls absorb a huge amount of time and effort. Undoing mistakes often involves raising additional capital that, because of the mistake, becomes harder and more expensive to raise.

Due diligence usually involves some desk research, but much more often it involves meeting with the key constituencies of the proposed business – the suppliers, the banks and, in the case of the medical centres, the real estate agents – and getting feedback from them about the feasibility of the concept. You are taking time. If taking time means that you miss the first site, there is almost always a better one. As you collect information and refine your judgement, the first sites you saw often turn out to have been less than perfect.

All over the world there are businesses that close down soon after they open. Entrepreneurs often fail to recognize their indecent haste. They think they are doing the right thing. They are unaware that analysis is possible. Or they worry about other people stealing their idea. Due diligence can be done a piece at a time without revealing the idea completely.

The risk of an idea being copied quickly is, in my experience, low: the world is sceptical about new ideas in general and large companies suffer from the not-invented-here syndrome, so they are generally unlikely to act until the concept is well and truly proven.

Rushing in is not entrepreneurship. At Apax we had a disciplined process for preparing investment proposals. We ensured that we had the necessary information about the product, the market, the competition, the management and the financing. In every

The first bounce
of the ball
everyone can see.
To anticipate
the second
you need
a really deep
understanding
of the market

investment proposal we had a section on the imponderables, so that we could isolate those aspects that were unknown or unquantifiable. For example, we might not know how the competition would respond. We would therefore isolate that aspect and focus on it. Eventually, we would have assessed all the ponderables and considered the imponderables as far as possible.

Ideally, it was only then that we made a decision. When you analyse an idea for a completely new enterprise you never achieve certainty that it will be successful. At best you'll be 60 per cent sure or 70 per cent sure of success. Sometimes, in competitive situations, we had to make a move when the situation was not completely clear. But we never made a decision impulsively, without putting in a great deal of work. If we needed to move quickly, we put more people on the job.

Do your homework, do not jump to conclusions, understand the trends, know where you are in the cycle – for your sector and for the economy as a whole – and always try to focus on the next bounce of the ball and how you can take advantage of it.

The first bounce of the ball everyone can see. To anticipate the second requires a really deep understanding of the market.

5

LEADING
A WINNING TEAM

Adapt your role
to the needs of the firm,
not the other
way round.

The nature of entrepreneurial strategy, like the nature of military strategy, resides in a combination of skills that are all brought to bear at the same time. You can easily teach the simple technical skills to do with financial analysis, modelling and accounting; it is much harder to teach the higher skills of entrepreneurship. Dr Johnson said that you can give somebody an argument but you cannot give them an understanding. Nor can you teach good judgement. In business, you can explain why things need to be done, but a full understanding only comes, if it comes at all, when the entrepreneur is able to relate the lesson to his or her own experience.

You cannot teach someone how to recruit a great team; you can only make them aware that recruiting a great team is what they have to do. You cannot teach someone how to recognize great talent, or how to judge if a particular person will be a good fit within a particular firm.

One of the many lessons I have learned in my career is that extremely bright, hard-working, talented entrepreneurs, with many of the qualities that I enumerated in chapter two, nevertheless make mistakes. They may have a great idea, but a mistaken business model. They may have a great model, but mistaken assumptions about capital intensity. They may have a terrific product, but mistaken ideas about the market. The most common mistake of all is that they underestimate the importance – and the difficulty – of bringing together the talents required to turn their vision into reality. Some entrepreneurs think that they are the only really important member of the team. Others suffer from poor judgement of people. Many – the weak entrepreneurs, not the strong ones – are threatened by the thought of recruiting someone as good as or better than themselves, and they shy away from doing so.

It can be tough to hire someone of really high calibre, who is an expert in his or her field, who has high expectations and who will make a demanding colleague. But that is what you have to do. As business guru Jim Collins has pointed out, 'Good is the enemy of great': if you start off recruiting people who are merely good, great people will not join the team.

The lesson of this chapter is that unless you recognize and recruit great people, and unless you are able to fashion a great team, you will not build a great organization and outdistance your competitors.

Phil Hulme and Peter Ogden at Computacenter built an outstanding team. At the time when the British economy was in a poor state at the end of the 1980s, a few of our investors put pressure on us to sell our stake in Computacenter. Sometimes your investors want you to do things without understanding the situation as well as you do and you have to be able to withstand that pressure. We withstood the pressure because we believed in the team. The company met a succession of challenges and thrived.

Phil and Peter – the former had been at Boston Consulting Group while the latter had been at Morgan Stanley – recruited outstanding people. By astute recruitment, they were able to scale up the business and keep running it efficiently. Phil was superb at that. Peter was the outward-facing one; Phil was the one who ran the operation. They had an excellent, broad-based management team with real strength in depth.

In 1991, my partner Maurice Tchénio backed a terrific management team that was running a small French cosmetics retailer, Shop-8, but which was capable of running a much larger operation. They took the company from eight stores to more than seventy through the acquisition of Sephora, a subsidiary of Boots, the British retailer. Sephora converted to the Shop-8 concept while all the outlets were rebranded as Sephora. We eventually sold the chain to luxury goods firm Louis Vuitton Moet Hennessy (LVMH) and made a profit of five times our investment.

Tim Waterstone presents a different approach to becoming a successful entrepreneur. A gifted strategist who was less interested in day-to-day management, Tim recruited a team that was able to find good sites, get the stores fitted out, open them quickly, maintain momentum and build market share. He was never the man to enjoy running a large organization day to day.

Ron James at PPL Therapeutics, the company that created Dolly the sheep, was different again. He failed to recruit and lead a team capable of exploiting the company's leading technology. We floated PPL on the London Stock Exchange in 1998 on the back of Dolly's creation, with an IPO value of $78 million. But Ron led the company into a number of failed ventures and left in 2002. His successors tried to save the company by selling off various patents to their competitors, shedding jobs, closing down some lines of research and spinning off others. It was too late. The board of directors resigned, the management team quit, and in September 2003 the advisory firm KPMG was brought in to find a buyer for the company's assets. The share price had dropped from 460 pence at flotation to 5.75 pence.

An entrepreneur in the right place (although possibly not quite at the right time – PPL was way ahead of the market) had missed what might have been a major opportunity to build a world-class company.

The first deciding factor in recruitment is not about the person you are hiring, it is about what you, the entrepreneur, are offering. Your first and most important offer is your vision. If you want to build a major firm you cannot do it by having a modest vision. All good entrepreneurs build towards a large scale from the beginning. They do not allow themselves to get bogged down in the minutiae of running a small business. If they did that, the business would stay small. Rather, they are guided by an inspiring vision, one that motivates them and informs all their decisions. It is this vision that initially attracts talented people to come and work with them.

If you start, say, a publishing business and you recruit bright, young people who are inexpensive, have little or no work experience and, despite their love of books, have little aptitude for business, you are not going to achieve a great deal. The calibre of the team will limit the scope of the business. If you want to get beyond that, you have to recruit a better team. But how do you attract people of high calibre to a business that is small, has a team of average quality and, as a result, cannot immediately afford to pay the market rate for the best talent? At what point do you decide that you need to recruit higher-calibre people than the ones you have already? How does your existing team react to the idea of recruiting a real star?

It is the scope of your vision that dictates the need for people of a certain calibre and it is also the scope of the vision that attracts those people. The vision excites the talent; the talent is attracted to the idea of achieving the vision.

If you are recruiting a finance director and you say to the candidate, 'Come and join this small publishing company that occupies a niche in the market,' you are going to attract a person of limited talent. If you say to the candidate, 'We are going to build the best publishing company of its type in the world, and this is how . . .' you are going to attract a person of a higher calibre. An inspiring but realistic vision (it has to be both) motivates people of high calibre to join you.

If there is a perceived gap between the aspiration and what might normally be considered a realistic level of achievement, it might be bridged by the faith that people have in your personal qualities or track record. When Sir Stelios Haji-Ioannou set up low-cost Easy-Cruise, people in the cruise business probably thought, 'Well, budget cruising sounds a bit of a contradiction in terms, but he has been an outstandingly successful entrepreneur, he built EasyJet and EasyCar, maybe he will be equally successful in the cruise business.' After only two years of operation, the jury is still out, but EasyCruise's no-frills approach seems to be working.

People have got to believe that you can reach your objective. As the leader, you have got to be convincing when you say, 'Come, we can do this together.'

The second thing you offer is leadership. If you are a leader, you will attract people who believe in your ability to lead them to success. The people who joined me at Apax thought that they would be more successful working with me than they would be working on their own. A star candidate is making an assessment of you and your business in an interview, just as much as you are making an assessment of him or her. 'Does this entrepreneur have an exciting vision? Is it a large opportunity? Is it a powerful business model? Is this entrepreneur capable of delivering his vision? Has he got, or is he likely to recruit, a great team?' He or she then probably considers, 'Have I got anything to offer this entrepreneur, and, if I have, can he take me further than I can go on my own?' What the candidate is looking for when he meets you is a leader, a person with entrepreneurial flair, with the ability to identify the opportunity, the courage to seize it and the skill to execute it. A leader, moreover, whom he or she can trust and with whom it would be enjoyable to work.

The third factor is the type of organization you are building. Most entrepreneurial businesses start out with a wheel structure, with the entrepreneur at the centre of the wheel and each member of the team reporting directly to him or her. This type of organization has two implications. First, it cannot cope with a staff of more than, say, forty people. Second, it greatly limits the calibre of person you can attract and retain.

Talented people will not generally join an organization where nothing happens unless the person at the centre approves it. These organizations are not only highly dependent upon the talent of one individual, they also face huge succession problems, because there is no other person in the organization of sufficient talent and leadership skill to take over when the founding entrepreneur retires or moves on.

At a certain point in the development of the firm, the founder must adapt, from being the sole decision-maker to being the leader of a team of decision-makers. If you are the entrepreneur, you have to realize that the day-to-day business has to be run by people who are better at their jobs than you would be. Your own job is then to steer the business dynamically in the right direction and to lead the management team effectively. If you resist that change, your business will suffer. This is why I say that the founder must adapt to the needs of the firm, not the other way round.

There was a time, in the early years of creating Apax, when I characterized myself driving alone in an open-top sports car. I recruited the first employee and he sat next to me. Then I recruited more, and they sat in the back. Then I recruited more and soon I had a car full of people. Before I knew it, it began to feel as if I was out of the car, pushing it uphill with all my team inside.

It was Rhys Williams, who joined Apax as a partner in 1984 from his position as CEO of GEC-Marconi, a very large company, who pointed out to me that it was necessary to develop my ideas on team management. I needed to change the way the company operated; to organize it so as to make it less dependent upon me for every decision. Unless I changed my role, we were going to get stuck. Over a period of time, I introduced Monday-morning meetings, sector teams with their own leaders and a number of key committees to deal with investment approvals, exits and operations. I ceased to be the hub; instead I became the leader, moving from the centre to the front of an organization structured in such a way that leaders of industry teams and operational committees organized themselves and made numerous decisions without consulting me. My role was then to provide leadership, in the sense of motivation and direction, and management of the industry team and committee leaders. My moving from the centre to the front was necessary for the firm to make a step-change in size while maintaining performance.

Identifying the most talented people, persuading them to join you, and leading an organization that empowers them, are three core skills for an entrepreneur. The moment you put the right person in a senior position, you feel it. The load on you is significantly reduced.

As you grow, there are other adjustments that need to be made in the way you manage the business. You start with a small number of people each doing multiple tasks. Then you have to shift to increasing specialization. In the early years, the finance director does administration, personnel and compliance, as well as finance. By the time you have grown to a decent size, you are going to have four or more people doing those jobs. So you have a changing organizational structure, which involves picking new people, and sometimes having to separate yourself from those with whom you started out.

Every time you pick somebody new there is a chance that the choice will turn out to be a bad one. Your organization will spend time and effort to make that person a productive member of the team. If he or she soon moves elsewhere, you have wasted all that effort. This is why I have always viewed a recruitment decision as an investment decision. It has a cost, a level of risk and, if it works, a great reward. If you are good at it, you will make few mistakes and you will move forward quickly.

When I started out in the 1970s, business textbooks were all about management theory: how to be a great manager. All business-school graduates were looking to be managers. It was the era of the large corporation and the multinational enterprise. At that time, entrepreneurship was still mostly a mystery.

Recently, as entrepreneurship has begun to emerge as a profession and a viable career option – prompted in significant part by the activities of private-equity firms – people have started crossing over into entrepreneurship from big-company management. This

Every recruitment decision is an investment decision: it has a cost, a level of risk, and, if it works, a great reward

includes senior people for whom entrepreneurship was not really an option when they started their working lives.

The situation has changed so much that it is now almost expected that senior managers will join private-equity firms, buy-outs or new ventures at some stage in their careers. This trend has become so marked today that if you are a manager and have not been approached to do a buy-out by the age of forty you begin to worry: perhaps you are not perceived to be as good as you think you are. The most successful executives in large companies are constantly being approached to join buy-out teams where they have a prospect of achieving real ownership and making real capital. We have shifted from having to persuade Rhys Williams in 1984 to leave GEC-Marconi to join Apax – the first such senior appointment in a European private-equity firm – to droves of senior executives moving to private-equity houses and the companies they back.

Senior management executives in large companies are thinking, 'If I get to the top of my organization, I will make a good salary but I will never accumulate real capital. I will go and join a new venture or a buy-out team. Forget the security. My salary will come down to half of what it is now, but I will have a good prospect of making serious capital.'

This is mostly one-way traffic. Few executives go back. In the old days, the view was that if you went into enterprise, you sacrificed security. But with ICI, Rolls-Royce, Courtaulds and others having to make painful adjustments to changing conditions, the apparent security and prestige of large businesses – which throughout the period of my career have shed a huge number of jobs – has evaporated.

Having said that, you have to exercise careful judgement in picking people from larger firms. Sometimes you can aim too high. You might think, 'I need a finance director from a large company because he already knows the road that I want to travel'. But actually the function of a finance director in a large company involves much less rolling up of sleeves and doing the accounting than is the case in a small company. Your new finance director might not relish the prospect. In addition, the culture in a large company is not entre-preneurial; you might end up with somebody who does not fit with the entrepreneurial culture of your firm. He or she might prove to be an expensive failure. It is a difficult adjustment for a person to move from a big-company environment to an entrepreneurial one.

At Apax, we recruited a 'big company' finance director when his 'medium-sized company' predecessor retired after ten years. The new finance director came from a large British bank. In the first year, he did not know what had hit him. He was used to a highly structured environment where decisions were handed down and he was required to follow laid-down procedures. At Apax, he found a situation where he was given a series of objectives but had to define for himself how to achieve them. He was not given specific instructions. It took him a while to adjust to that. He had to change from being process-driven to being objective-driven.

A positive example was Dr Hamish Hale, who joined Apax in 1984, at about the same time as Rhys Williams. Hamish had been European head of research for G. D. Searle, the pharmaceutical company. He had heard about what we were doing and he thought that private equity could play a constructive role in healthcare and biotechnology. Unlike our new finance director, Hamish Hale adapted easily to the world of enterprise and early-stage ventures. He was with us for many years and was responsible for, among other things, our investment in PPL Therapeutics, the company that cloned Dolly the sheep.

In many cases, before you choose your employees you have to choose your partners. Today, most entrepreneurs work in partnership with their senior team members. But, as my experience demonstrates, choosing your partners has to be done carefully.

Entrepreneurship is a self-selecting profession. Two of our founding partners in MMG decided that it was not for them. The truth is that they were not entrepreneurial enough. When we were working together, one or other of them would always be in a severe state of doubt or depression. Every evening Maurice Tchénio and I had to build them up enough for them to feel confident about work the next day. We were all getting the same salary, making all decisions together. It was like being tied at the ankle running an eight-legged race.

We set up a business, we struggled, and two of the four partners found the going too tough and left. But far from being a disaster, this was an opportunity. I went into partnership with Alan Patricof and we emerged far, far stronger than we had been before.

Had I been less confident in my own ability, or less optimistic, or, indeed, had I a less accurate picture of the world in my head, I might never have called Alan Patricof. I might have gone back to employment and everything would have been different. What I was able to do instead was turn the problem into an opportunity. With Alan Patricof as a partner, we had a better base on which to build a great team.

An important aspect of building a business is that entrepreneurs crave a feeling of ownership and responsibility. They have to be in a position of leadership. If you are a frustrated entrepreneur in a number-two position, reporting to somebody who is not really implementing what you recommend, it will eat you up. If you are an entrepreneur with partners who are not pulling their weight or who are pulling in different directions, it will frustrate you. If you are an entrepreneurial employee you strive for a position of leadership and responsibility at your level, even if it involves saying to the person you are working for, 'Give me responsibility for getting this done and please let me do it on my own.'

If you are entrepreneurial you are hamstrung until you are in the position of a leader. It is not only because your colleagues are saying, 'You can't do that,' or 'It can't be done that way,' it is also because you do not own the challenge of building your part of the firm. That sense of ownership is what every entrepreneur finds fulfilling.

Partnerships can frustrate that: everything can be up for discussion and revision all the time. Seldom does everyone agree. It is not uncommon for partnerships to be negative in their effect, especially if the partners have similar skills, similar roles and an equal voice. There can be too much consensus, too much hiding behind the collective authority of the group. The partners have interesting and well-informed discussions, and possibly even come to the right conclusions more often than not. But because none of them is acting like an entrepreneur there is no one in charge, no leadership, and none of the decisions leads to decisive action. There is insufficient follow-through, insufficient execution.

There are few examples of true entrepreneurial partnerships. Teams, yes, but not partnerships of equals. Even the successful professional partnerships, such as law and accountancy firms, tend to have been built up by a clear leader – usually the person whose name is on the letterhead. Sometimes you get partnerships or management teams where one is the strategist and the other is the administrator, or one is the front man and the other is the operational or technical expert. Their relationship might be symbiotic, but only one of them is the leader.

Yet even for a leader there are certain activities that you can only carry out with partners of equal standing. Then it is important to define the nature of the partnership in such a way that each of you can continue to exercise leadership. It would have been impossible for me in the 1970s to have set up an office in the United States and recruited a great person to run it. I had no financial means to do it.

If the solution is partnership, it is often preferable to have something more like a federation, in which each office manages its own expansion, and all you share are cross-holdings, the brand and some back-office functions.

Because we ran independent operations – Alan Patricof in New York, Maurice Tchénio in Paris and me in London – we avoided most of the pitfalls of partnership. I was free to build the business as I thought fit. My operation worked differently from Alan's or Maurice's. When I left Apax in 2005, of the $20 billion under management, Alan and Maurice had $2 billion in each of their respective operations.

Why the big difference between my operation and theirs?

There is, of course, more than one factor involved. I was able to build on the unification of the national operations that Alan, Maurice and I had originally set up; the positions of France and Britain (the 'sick man of Europe' when we started out) had been reversed over three decades; Alan had resisted the move into buy-outs, preferring to concentrate on early-stage investment; and the intensity of competition was different in each market. But I believe that, fundamentally, the explanation is that I was able to attract the strongest team.

From 1990 until 2002, I had around me a senior group of half a dozen people in London: Peter Englander (who had joined me in 1981), Adrian Beecroft (1984), Clive Sherling (1987), John McMonigall (1990) and Toby Wyles (1990). Later, when we merged with our German operations, the head of the German office, Martin Halusa, became the seventh member of the group. When you get a team of really great people like that, working effectively together, the level of motivation is extremely high and progress and performance can be fantastic.

The seven senior executives were the pillars of the firm. Many other gifted members of the team were the crossbeams.

Creating the right entrepreneurial culture within a firm is a tough challenge; in entrepreneurial activity you need to empower people. Empowering people means that you have to let them get on with it, which means that you have to trust them, and trusting them means that you trust in their sense of responsibility: so that they say, when they are unsure or in difficulty, 'I need input over here.' You can build in checks and balances, but basically it is a question of empowerment and trust.

You also have to give people appropriate but powerful incentives. This can be a delicate matter, because, in business terms, not all people are of equal value. As the leader you cannot ignore that. If you pay each member of the staff the same, the one who knows he has the rarer and more marketable skills will get disenchanted. If pay differentials are too great, the one whose skills are admittedly more common – and who is therefore more easily replaced – complains that it is unfair and disrupts the harmony of the firm.

It is useful to be reminded in this context that all things happen because of multiple causation. When you strike a match, it is not only the sulphur, it is the act of striking, the presence of oxygen and the friction that ignite it. Power and value go to the rarer element. If there is plenty of oxygen but only one match, the match clearly has a higher value than the oxygen, even though both are required.

Sometimes people ignore this fact. Because they are necessary to an enterprise they sometimes think they are equally valuable to it. They are not. It is a crucial distinction.

When many people are sitting around the table, it is clear that one person has rarer skills than another. They are all essential – as is the person who cleans the office – but there is a different market for each of them, there is a rarity value. The star, the striker, usually has the most value.

In partnerships and in management you have to give people a sense of their strengths, their contribution to the firm and their rarity value. So that when someone comes in and asks for a role that is unsuitable or they ask for remuneration that is not commensurate with their role, you can get them to understand how they fit into the wider perspective of the business.

Without doubt, if you have a star – and you should be looking to recruit stars – you have to pay them handsomely. You have to be sure that they get a good share of the value created by their performance. If you do not, either they will cease to perform or they will build their own value and move across to a higher bidder or to start a firm of their own.

You should be cultivating a culture in your firm where the rewards of success are shared fairly and appropriately. The first generation of leaders at Apax, who left at about the same time or shortly before I did, made a considerable financial sacrifice so that the new generation could convert to a formal partnership structure, which we felt would give better continuity to the firm. I have never had the attitude of holding on to all the profit. A big share of a small pie is of no interest. My role model was Marvin Bower, who gave away some of his own shares to ensure the greater success of McKinsey.

It took me until 1990 to assemble the core Apax team. Before the launch of each fund, I added people. If I added right, I did well. If I added wrong, then I took a step back as people left. I had two partners leave in the mid-1980s. The first was Rhys Williams, who went back to join the board of GEC-Marconi. He was a brilliant manager of large businesses. The other was Peter Troughton, who went off to run the hospitals of New Zealand. He had joined me from BT, and he, too, loved large organizations and thrived on managing them.

It was Peter, as he left, who recommended John McMonigall to me as his successor, to head our telecommunications team. John turned out to be a spectacular investor. The interesting thing about him is that his first investment, The Red Telephone Company, went bad and, if he or we had lost confidence, he could have left the firm at that stage. But he was sure he would be successful, persevered, and went on to have a tremendous record, paying back three funds out of his investments alone: that is to say that the success of the investments for which he personally was responsible was equal to the value of the three funds as a whole. The investments for which the rest of the team were responsible added profits on top.

In seeking to attract the best people to the team, what should you be looking for? Should you be looking for people who are not going to be entrepreneurs in their own right? Or are you looking for people who might work best with responsibility for their own area?

The answer at Apax is that I tended to look for all-rounders who were entrepreneurial, but were also team players. Executives in private equity have to be able not only to analyse opportunities alone, but also to make decisions that benefit from being a member of a team. They also need to have the personality to persuade entre-preneurs to change the way they do things. In private equity you have to be financially trained and to have an understanding of management, but you also have to have a strategic brain while being sensitive to tactical and people issues.

I always tried to recruit the best talent possible. I tried to recruit John Burgess (who went on to lead BC Partners, which has had a great track record to date) and Mike Smith (who now heads up CVC, which is one of the biggest competitors to Apax today). I recruited Jon Moulton, who had led Schroder Ventures and later set up Alchemy Partners.

You cannot build a successful firm that is decentralized in its decision-making and its deal-generation, without having entrepreneurial people heading different parts of its operations. You benefit greatly in this respect from maintaining the continuity of a talented team. The team develops an ability to learn from its collective experience. The members of the team can speak in shorthand, as it were, about investment opportunities and problems, and can calibrate situations according to benchmarks that have been arrived at through collective experience.

My own starting point at Apax was something close to the film *The Dirty Dozen*, which told the story of a group of tough individualists with complementary skills, who come together to achieve the most challenging of wartime missions. I recommend that film to any budding entrepreneur.

The Apax team comprised former consultants, executives from big business, executives from technology backgrounds and people with high-level financial skills. Some were good at protecting the downside; others were good at identifying and capturing the upside.

Peter Englander had been at Boston Consulting Group, as had Adrian Beecroft. Clive Sherling joined us from Arthur Andersen. John McMonigall came from a senior position at BT. Toby Wyles came from Morgan Stanley. They were all entrepreneurial. None of them would have joined if they had not felt that Apax offered an entrepreneurial opportunity to build a first-rate firm and make significant capital in the process.

Life at Apax was not always easy. When the economy was strong it was exciting, at other times it could be nerve-wracking. The recession in the early 1990s was a really tough period. Just as stressful in a way was the hi-tech bubble at the end of that decade. We proved that we could seize the opportunities when they presented themselves, and batten down the hatches when necessary.

When we started to run the first fund in 1981, our office was in Upper Grosvenor Street, in London's Mayfair. I had a first-floor office and Peter Englander, Joanna Armandias (both still at Apax) and the rest of the team were working in the basement. My father was cheerfully there too. He had closed his textile business in 1979 and I had immediately invited him to help us. He ran finance and administration for many years. In 1984, as we raised the second fund, we moved to a larger office around the corner in Upper Brook Street. When we raised the fourth fund in 1990, I decided to buy rather than rent. We bought a building in Portland Place, in London's West End, in 1991. My father occupied an office next to mine and it was a pleasure for us to work together until his death in 1997.

Number fifteen Portland Place is an elegant building in an elegant street. To me a building is more than just space. It is a marketing message about your brand. You get to the stage in a growing business where, instead of going out to make every sale, business starts to come to you. That is the point at which marketing starts to become more important than selling. It is the beginning of building a brand. Building a brand is the fourth key element, after vision, leadership and the type of organization, in attracting the best recruits.

We reached that stage at Apax in the early 1990s. By 1993, when the results of the recession-hit 1990 funds were not looking encouraging, I brought in professional skills to build the brand in a systematic way.

We needed articles in the press. We needed to produce publications looking at interesting aspects of the sector. We used advertising. Every time we completed a transaction, we placed what is called a tombstone advertisement: a simple announcement of the deal with the transaction value highlighted in the text. When we announced that we had backed Chris Evans in the acquisition of Virgin Radio, we not only took an advertisement on the front page of the Companies & Markets section of the *Financial Times*, we added a cartoon. It was a way of attracting attention and raising awareness of our firm and its activities ahead of a fundraising. Partly as a result of these efforts, our 1995 fundraising was a great success.

The power of a brand in private equity is that it attracts entrepreneurs, investors and talent. If you do not have a brand you cannot get the best people. I could get the best people because the firm was deemed to have a personality. It was well known, it was not flamboyant, it had strong values, it was associated with quality and uniqueness – which is the meaning of Apax in ancient Greek. (The Apax name is thus both an extension of the acronym for Alan Patricof Associates and a meaningful word in its own right.) We were the only private-equity firm spanning early stage and buy-outs, across five different sectors, including high technology, on a multinational basis.

As part of the brand-building exercise at Apax, I wanted a building that looked like the headquarters of a substantial organization with significant capital. Number fifteen Portland Place fitted the bill.

If you had walked through our offices in 1975, we would have had five people, including backroom staff. In 1981, we would have had

144

about fifteen. In 1984, it might have been twenty-five. In 1987, thirty to forty. In 1990, forty to sixty. In 1999, I sold the corporate-finance advisory business with which I had started, thereby reducing the head-count temporarily. By 2005, we had merged our American operation, which employed fifty people, with the 250 people in the European and Israeli operations, which I led. This took us to around three hundred. Maurice in Paris added another seventy.

I lost very few people in the course of my Apax career. You can count them on the fingers of one hand. I have never lost anyone to the competition whom I wanted to keep. I believe in stability as the basis for growth.

I have followed the principle of what some nineteenth-century political theorists called the 'inevitability of gradualness'. In a field where continuity of experience and personnel is important – so that, for example, investors can see that expertise is entrenched in the firm – you do things gradually and thoughtfully. You do not dissipate your expertise by letting experienced people wander off to the competition, nor do you act precipitously in the hope that you can adjust the skills of your team by ruthless firings.

Fear and uncertainty make for a bad corporate culture: your best people begin to wonder about their own positions in the firm and start looking for opportunities to jump ship.

Having said that, there is no point implementing a culture of continuity if you employ weak people. That would be self-defeating. You have to employ people with great potential, and have the people and the firm grow together. In other words, you recruit the best people from the start, people who share your vision, and you make it attractive for them to stay in the firm.

Whenever someone did leave, I used the principle of

Whenever someone leaves, use it as an opportunity to get someone better

leapfrogging – of using their departure as an opportunity to get someone better. In losing somebody, you have removed a constraint on your progress. It is an opportunity to move forward faster. I learned that lesson from the departure of my original partners in MMG.

The fifth factor in recruitment, after vision, leadership, organizational culture and brand, is success. The best people are attracted to the most successful businesses. In British retail, the giant supermarket chain Tesco will get better people than anybody else, because it seems to have the best leadership, the best track record and the most successful model.

People say: 'That is the company I want to join, that is where I want to build my career.' Tesco can attract and pick from the best. By recruiting the best, it secures its continuing success. It is a virtuous circle.

As an entrepreneur, you will be successful to the degree that you can attract the best talent to your team.

You attract the best talent by offering vision and leadership, by delegating to and trusting your colleagues, by creating a culture of empowerment within the firm and a sense of obligation to it, by providing appropriate incentives to maintain the continuity of your team, by building a great brand and by being successful. Ultimately, the difference between you and your competitors comes down to one factor only: the talent of your team.

Ultimately, the difference between you and your competitors comes down to one factor only: the talent of your team

6

SMART MONEY

Don't just raise cash,
raise your probability
of success.

Good entrepreneurs develop a kind of X-ray vision. They can see through all the operational issues – the products, the markets, the clients and the staff – down to the hard, underlying financial structure of their business. It is like seeing the skeleton under the flesh. As an entrepreneur and manager, you will concern yourself with that skeleton, as it becomes visible through the profit and loss account, the cash-flow statement and the balance sheet.

The first and most pressing financial issue concerns the initial capital investment, and the cash still available: do you have the funds you need to fulfil your business-plan targets?

All too often, inexperienced entrepreneurs underestimate the resources they will need, the time it will take to get to market and the time it will take for their product to become established.

You might believe, for instance, that your new product will be launched within a year. But getting a new product into the market is difficult. You might be too optimistic. Suppose it takes longer than a year? Suppose you are halfway through your product development, you have no clients and you have run out of money? No matter how good the concept or how brilliant the design, if it does not get to market it is of no value.

You must have enough capital to carry your venture through the planned stages of its development and to provide a prudent contingency for delays and unforeseen setbacks.

There is a temptation – indeed, there can be a constant pressure – to understate the amount of funding required for your venture. Investors want to provide the minimum to guarantee success. Everyone wants to keep the funding requirement low.

This can be the worst mistake to make. Think of capital as a runway and think of your firm as a plane ready to take off. It is no use heading down the tarmac only to find, just as you are picking up speed, that the runway is not long enough for take-off.

Too often, entrepreneurs underestimate the length of the runway, either because it is tough to raise a larger amount, or because they do not want to give away too large a share in the company to the financiers, or because they have insufficient experience and are too optimistic about the capital required. Whatever the reason, they find themselves running out of runway just when they are close to take-off.

The rules of the entrepreneurial game are that if you run out of cash and the business is not yet able to fund itself, you either shut up shop or you go out and find fresh investment. Raising more money under these circumstances is generally extremely costly – because, essentially, you are asking investors to rescue you.

**You don't want
to discover
you need
more runway
just when you
are picking up
speed**

Let us say your original investors put up $4 million for a 40 per cent stake and that this valued the company at $6 million before the money was invested and $10 million after. Let us say that because the business had insufficient capital at the outset it has not performed as you expected and you now need an additional $2 million. You are able to find new investors but this time at a lower price – reflecting your lack of success. Let us say that you agree terms whereby you have to issue 50 per cent more shares, so that the new investors purchase 33.3 per cent of the company. This now values your venture, after the investment of the new money, at $6 million.

In other words, where before the company was valued at $10 million after the original money had been raised and you owned 60 per cent, it is now worth, after the addition of the new cash, only $6 million and your 60 per cent stake has been diluted to 40 per cent. Your initial investors no longer own 40 per cent, they own 26.7 per cent. The new round of finance has not been raised at a premium to the original value (which is always the ideal); it has been raised at a discount to the initial value. Yet the underlying proposition might be just as good as it ever was. It might even be better, given the investment already made and the experience that you have accumulated in the meantime.

If you fail again and you have to raise yet more capital, you and your first investors will again suffer a 'haircut' on your shares of the company.

You could have avoided all these problems if you had taken an entrepreneurial investor through your plan and raised the money you really needed – the initial $4 million plus the additional $2 million – in the first place. You might then have raised the $6 million at the original $6 million pre-money valuation and let go of 50 per cent of the shares, leaving you with 50 per cent. You would thereby have saved yourself valuable time, pain, effort and anxiety – because if you stop when you are halfway down the runway, it invariably takes an enormous effort to get started again – as well as securing an appropriate share of a properly capitalized company.

So, it is crucial for the entrepreneur to manage the financial dimension of his or her venture from the beginning. As far as investment capital is concerned, this means, essentially, raising neither too much nor too little at each stage of the game. But if you are going to err, err on the side of raising too much. Almost invariably, entrepreneurs err on the side of raising too little. This only increases the likelihood of failure and ends up costing more.

While nearly all businesses need capital, that does not mean that they all need capital in the form of equity. Sometimes you can cleverly finance a new business entirely with debt. Two young entrepreneurs came in to see me one day. They had the idea of establishing a business by putting advertisements on the back of rest-room doors. They needed to raise some money. They said: 'We think we need $600,000 or $800,000 of equity investment to get this off the ground.' I listened and then asked: 'Is it really necessary to raise equity? Think about your business model.'

Many people do not think seriously about their business model – that is, the elements of their business that drive its profitability, cash-flows and growth. They think only about their product and their operations. Here the product was advertising space on the backs of doors in rest rooms. It sounds like a limited market, a niche, but maybe it was capable of wider application. After all, we have advertising in bus shelters, and this has become a large market.

I pointed out to them that, looking at it from a financial point of view, their business model was one where they were going to lock in some bankable relationships at the start: they were going to sign

"THESE FIGURES CAN BE MISLEADING,
SO I WILL ATTEMPT TO CLARIFY
THEM THROUGH THE USE OF
INTERPRETIVE DANCE."

Bill Whitehead drew this cartoon in the early 1990s, when virtually no company in our portfolio was on plan and the management teams found it increasingly difficult to present their progress or their prospects with any confidence.

154

leases for doors with companies that owned shopping centres, petrol stations and suchlike who are highly credible with banks, and they were going to sign long-term contracts with credible advertisers.

If they could get some of the major retailers and service stations to grant them leases and if they could get just a few advertisers to commit to taking space on those doors, then they could go to the bank, having calculated their revenue expectations and their costs, and ask the bank to lend money against this, to provide all the cash to launch their operation. That way they could raise the working capital in the form of debt and sell zero equity.

That is what they did. Instead of raising $600,000 to $800,000 worth of equity, which might have entailed selling about one-third of the business, they borrowed the money from the bank. Within two years their cash flow had enabled them to pay off the bank and they owned 100 per cent of the business with no debt outstanding. They now have more than 25,000 advertising panels in motorway service stations, shopping centres, bars, nightclubs and health clubs.

Whatever form your first-round finance takes it should be sufficient to achieve lift-off. It should take you to a predicted, much-improved situation – preferably, but not necessarily, operating profits – at which you are able to demonstrate the validity of the idea, the scale of the opportunity, the competence of your team and the receptiveness of the market. At that stage, investors will be keen to invest in the company; you should expect to raise a second round of finance at a substantially higher valuation than the first. To continue with our earlier hypothetical example, perhaps you raise an additional $5 million at a pre-money valuation of $30 million. The additional $5 million commands a 14.3 per cent stake of a company now valued at $35 million post-money. You are left with just under 43 per cent of the shares worth $15 million, whereas your original 50 per cent stake was worth $6 million. Your share of the company has been diluted but your stake has increased in value.

If you are dealing with the uncertainties of start-up businesses, the best approach is often to say, 'There are three milestones in getting this product out. I am going to raise enough money now, before I start, to get me to the second milestone. Then when I get to the first milestone, I will raise more to get me to the third milestone.' And so on. That way you have a much lower financing risk profile.

Where do you go for the money? One place to go today is to the private-equity firms, especially to the venture capitalists among them.

During my years at Apax we invested in about 2 per cent of the early-stage proposals that were offered to us. We must have evaluated fifteen thousand serious proposals, each of which had an entrepreneur and a business plan. With all that experience under my belt, can I spot a potentially successful entrepreneur when he or she first walks through the door? Do the ones who are going to make it have an identifiable quality? And if they do, are those qualities discernible only in the 2 per cent and not in the rest?

Well, there are certain qualities that are common to the 2 per cent – and, indeed, to the other entrepreneurs whom we turned down but whom other private-equity houses backed. But of that 2 per cent, maybe two out of every ten will be huge successes. So it is not 2 per cent, it is really about 0.4 per cent of all those would-be entrepreneurs who are really going to achieve something outstanding.

As to the rest of the 2 per cent, probably two in ten are likely to be failures. This may have nothing to do with the calibre of the entrepreneur. It is liberating to understand that failure is not always your own fault. It could be that the market has unexpectedly changed, the competition has come up with something completely different that renders your product less attractive, the business cycle has taken an unforeseen downturn, or the government has imposed a regulation that makes your trade less profitable. The fact that we backed entrepreneurs and ideas that failed shows that their faults were not obvious. To us, they looked like they were going to be successful. As the Book of Ecclesiastes says, the race is not always to the swift. You do not have total control of the elements that determine the success of your enterprise. Even the best entrepreneurs can fail for reasons beyond their control.

The remainder – the six out of every ten we backed – are likely to be neither outstanding successes nor failures. They are mostly the 'good enough' companies, although this category covers a wide spectrum of performance, from mediocre to very good.

In any event, about 70 to 80 per cent of early-stage proposals backed by venture firms are likely to be successful to some degree. This proves, among other things, how carefully we choose our investments. It does not mean we do not make mistakes. Not only did about 20 per cent of our investments at Apax in my time lose money, but we inevitably rejected some proposals that went on to be successful elsewhere.

In your first meeting with a private-equity firm what will the investors be looking for? The largest part of the decision in the first meeting is probably going to be based on your credibility as an entrepreneur and on the credibility of your business plan.

Some businesses are almost wholly reliant on the calibre of the people involved. Examples would be investment banks, advertising agencies and film and television production companies. When you invest in those businesses you invest in the people, nothing else. It is

WOW! THIS SAYS "THERE'S ALWAYS SOMETHING NEW UNDER THE SUN, THE TRICK IS NOT TO GET BURNT...FINDING IT."

By 1999, the market for raising capital for hi-tech ventures was so hot it was dangerous. Anything that ended in dot.com commanded a ridiculously high valuation – and some private-equity investor would invariably pay for it.

one of the reasons why such investments are, by and large, unpopular in the private-equity community.

Other businesses have assets other than talent. Examples would be property, traditional manufacturing, retailing and distribution businesses. The entrepreneur at the helm is still crucially important, but the technical and creative challenges of the business are less dependent on individual talent. When you invest in a real estate venture you can reasonably expect to end up owning property of some value, even if the entrepreneur proves to be a disappointment. When you invest in a television production business, you may end up with nothing at all.

If I were looking at a proposal for a television business or an advertising agency, my initial response would be almost entirely based on the calibre of the entrepreneur. If I were looking at a property opportunity, I would probably concentrate more evenly on the market, the cycle, the business model and the plan, as well as the entrepreneur.

The remaining part of my judgement would be based on factors to do with the balance of our portfolio and market conditions.

As to the qualities we are hoping to find in the entrepreneur, we are always trying to work out whether somebody can be outstandingly successful. That judgement is mostly a function of whether the person has a successful track record, whether he or she is realistic about the way the world works, and whether they have sufficiently broad skills to be able to attract talented executives and to run the business in a responsible way.

As well as the positive traits we are looking for, there are negative traits we are hoping to avoid: the false, seductive attributes that you learn to identify and to treat with caution. A central question is always: 'Is this person just a good salesman or is there a serious opportunity here? If there is a serious opportunity, is this the person to make the most of it?' There are many people with forceful personalities who can dress themselves up to look credible. Investors have learned to be careful. The way a private-equity firm deals with this is by checking with the person's previous employers, clients, suppliers and even competitors. The impression you make in the first meeting needs to be positive enough for the venture capitalist to think, 'I should make several telephone calls to find out more about this person.'

When people meet you they are assessing you at two levels, at an intellectual level and at an intuitive level. They are listening to you but they are also observing you. From their observation they are trying to assess your ability to do the things you are telling them. They are asking themselves: 'Can this person really attract good people?' or, 'Does this person have someone on their team who has a really good grasp of the financial dimension?' Sometimes you have a meeting with an entrepreneur who may be very bright and have made an excellent case for the venture, but you just know that he or she could not fight their way out of a paper bag. They are just not practical; they are good at thinking but they are not good at doing. That comes across in ways that are often intuitive.

Investors need to know that you have what it takes. You have to impress upon them that you can deliver, that you will succeed. Track record is important. Your personal commitment and conviction is important. Evidence that you have or can recruit a capable team that believes in you is important.

Crucially, you cannot pretend to be someone you are not. You will be found out. If you are a thinker and the situation needs an implementer, make sure you get someone on your side of the table who has a proven track record in implementation.

Your track record is a determinant for the venture-capital industry. There will always be people who have been failures in the past, who have learned from those experiences and who turn round to become massive successes subsequently. But they are the exception and, although venture capitalists are very much aware that exceptions are sometimes the way to great returns, the rule tends to be that people who have performed well and enjoy good reputations will continue to perform well and enjoy good reputations.

In any event, experienced investors will definitely speak to people with whom the entrepreneur has worked before. This is an important part of their due diligence process.

When you enquire about a person, you get a range of reactions. You never get a 100 per cent accurate or consistent picture, but within a range of 20 per cent or 30 per cent of variability you can get a good idea of that person's strengths and weaknesses.

People might say about someone, 'He is the smartest person I have ever worked for, he is of undoubted integrity, but he may be a bit academic, rather than practical.' That does not mean you eliminate that person. More likely you would ask: 'Is this person capable of attracting people who are street-wise and who will follow him because of his skills and because they trust him?' If the answer is yes, you go for it. Such a person could be a great leader of the right team.

One of the key criteria in the first meeting is the degree of determination of the individual. Some people think that the notion that you have to be passionate about your project is just rhetoric, but it is not. If you are not completely persuaded, you will not be able to persuade anyone else. I can tell if someone is not really convinced; and if they are not convinced how likely are they to make it through the inevitable ups and downs of building a business?

The entrepreneur's passion, however, does not obviate the need for due diligence. Both are essential.

Then there are young entrepreneurs who have huge energy and determination but who lack people skills. People skills amount to a kind of intelligence and I am wary when that intelligence is missing. It is not uncommon among managers to find underdeveloped people skills. Businesses are the poorer for it, but generally they can get by. Among entrepreneurs, however, highly developed people skills are essential. A young entrepreneur without people skills can be a success, but the extent of that success will be limited. Such a person could run a business of, say, thirty people but not three hundred, because to do the latter he or she would have to bring in other people at a high level and, given his or her lack of people skills, that would be unlikely to happen. You could see them going so far down the track, but they could not go all the way.

From time to time you will find individuals who are very able, even though the opportunity they have identified is limited. You feel that they will either transform the opportunity or they will connect with a larger opportunity at some point; you therefore back them. I once interviewed an entrepreneur who wanted to create a business in controlled-circulation publishing. It was not a massive market but he was a good person to back, and I thought: 'Well, if he does not manage to develop this into a major business he will find something else. I would like to back him.' We made ten times our money on the investment.

You often get people approaching you with ideas that are only 50 per cent clear. They have taken into account their own particular skills, but they have not taken into account all the other attributes that a successful business needs. Or they may have decided that they need to get started come what may, and they have started where it is easiest to start. But, as I noted earlier, the places where it is easy to start tend to be relatively indefensible. They do not offer significant protection in the form of barriers against others doing the same thing.

When entrepreneurs come through the door they exhibit very different levels of self-confidence. Some will speak with a command of the facts and a cogent analysis of the opportunity and the risks. They do not boast, they do not prevaricate and they are not evasive. They may have high aspirations, but they talk straight, and convey that they have a realistic assessment of the difficulties that lie ahead. Others are on the defensive: they want to raise money for their business because if they do not they face a crisis. They therefore force themselves to appear optimistic. Sometimes they overdo it.

An entrepreneur came in to see me once wanting to raise money for a technical platform for investment management firms. This was not in fact the business he wanted to be in. He wanted to be in investment management itself. The technical platform was just his way of getting a foot in the door. Technical platforms for investment management firms have only so much value, certainly in comparison with the sort of firm he really wanted to build. But he felt that he had to start where it was easiest for him to start.

If you start in the wrong place, as the Irish joke has it, it is difficult to get to your destination.

He knew that by proposing one business as a stepping-stone to another he was on weak ground. He was going through the motions explaining the plan in increasingly confused detail and it made no sense at all. He eventually conceded that he knew that the plan he was putting to us was flawed.

This entrepreneur would have been better off dealing with the challenge head on and saying, 'I need help. I'm in the wrong business and I want to be some place else.' When I spoke with my colleagues after the meeting we agreed: 'This person will get bogged down in trying to build up a technical platform and is unlikely to gravitate from there to becoming a successful asset manager.'

This example raises the issue of the negotiating position. If the individual or the proposition lacks credibility, it is highly unlikely that the entrepreneur will secure the required investment. Furthermore, an entrepreneur lacking credibility is always on the defensive, which is a poor position from which to negotiate.

You cannot really negotiate well unless you put yourself in a position psychologically where you can walk away from the deal. There are so many situations where people have not thought through what their alternatives are; they are just desperate to do the deal whatever happens. In those circumstances, they cannot negotiate. They can only concede. I used to say to my colleagues, 'Let's think this through. How can we put ourselves in a position where we can walk away from this transaction – and the other side can credibly believe that we will walk away – if we don't get what we want?'

The same rule applies when the entrepreneur is trying to raise money from the private-equity investor. If you are desperate for the money and have nowhere else to go, you are not in a position to negotiate. The private-equity investor can dictate terms. This is not a position that any professional investor welcomes. It suggests that the entrepreneur is weak. Who would want to back a weak entrepreneur?

I would note here that deals are only made if both sides are better off having made the deal than they were before. The best outcome is when both sides are equally happy. Negotiation is about the balance of benefit. If you are a good negotiator, you will get more of the benefit. If the other side are better negotiators, they will get more.

But if either side gets to a position where it can see insufficient benefit, or where the benefit of the deal is less than the benefit of another deal, the deal will not happen and no amount of huffing and puffing will bring it back to the table.

There are two schools of thought here. One says that you should try to get the absolute maximum in every negotiation. The other says that it is better to aim for something that is realistic, even if that means leaving something on the table for the other side. I think the difference between these views is often a question of personality. Some people have the instinct always to get everything they can. They want every penny at every stage. There are others, perhaps more reasonable in nature, who go the other way: they try to get a fair deal done.

My own belief is that you are more likely to become successful if you try to do a fair deal, not an extortionate one. I think it is better to have a reputation for being effective and fair; for being a person with whom it is possible to do business. Bear in mind that relationships count; you do not want to lose the deal to the competition; you want to create the sense on the other side that you are going to be a good partner. To achieve this, you have to have a view of what you want and what is fair, to you as well as to the other side.

The first step in the negotiation stage is to present your proposal. Many times when people came to pitch for money at Apax it was as if they had stored up a recorded presentation in their heads and the first meeting was an outpouring of all they wanted to convey. Such presentations invariably proceeded at a fast pace, as if they hoped that they could sell us on the idea before we had a chance to draw breath. This is not an effective approach. Better to say, 'We have a whole presentation to show you, but perhaps you would like to tell us first what it is you are looking for.' If you approach the matter that way, you get the other party – in this case the prospective investor – to show their hand. You will then know what their concerns are and you can address those concerns during the hour or so that has been allotted for the meeting.

Once you know the other side's real concerns, you are able to address the point you are trying to get across more effectively.

I have been in a meeting where a colleague was pitching to a potential investor in one of our funds and the person on the other side started fidgeting. The reason was that my colleague had launched into his presentation, which would take twenty minutes or so, and the person he was addressing was not interested in the presentation. He was not worried about whether there was scope for another fund of this type. We did not need to take him through the market and the competition and the strategic factors. He assumed that we would not waste his time by having done anything other than thoroughly prepare our case. What he was worried about was whether we were going to succeed in recruiting the people required to achieve the necessary performance.

We should not have been boring him with our prepared message; we should have been finding out about the message he wanted to get across to us and addressing that as well.

In those kinds of meetings, it is better to shake the person's hand, look him or her in the eye, make a brief opening statement and quickly defer to him by asking the question: 'What is it that you are particularly interested in?' Throughout your presentation you pause and prompt the other person to react and to disclose their concerns.

It may not be possible to ascertain whether you have got the best deal without at some stage going beyond what the other side can accept. You have to be in a position where you can test them to the limit without causing offence and without jeopardizing the deal.

You want to be able to retrieve the situation, if necessary, without appearing to back down. In a sense, it is a question of judging how far to go 'too far'. This requires you to listen closely to what the other side is thinking. Sometimes people only tell you what they are thinking on the doorstep as they leave. In my experience, the last thing to be said is generally the most significant.

As an investor, in the first meeting with an entrepreneur I try to be passive and let them set out their stall. I learned to my cost that if you infuse too much of yourself into somebody else's vision or business plan you will overstate its potential. What you are doing is substituting yourself for the entrepreneur and selling yourself on the investment opportunity.

You want the entrepreneur to describe his or her idea as fully as possible. Then you question its detail and see what reaction you get, to work out whether or not you have got somebody here who has a robust view and a grasp of detail. You might come out of the meeting saying, 'You know what, there is the germ of an idea here but this person is never going to do it. He is never going to come up with the right business model, he is never going to attract the right executives, he does not understand the financial dimension. Forget it.' Or you might say, 'The idea looks promising but it needs a lot of work. Fortunately, this entrepreneur seems dynamic as well as level-headed. Let us ask her to refine the idea and let us set a date for a second meeting.'

Subsequent meetings have to do with refining the idea, because even great entrepreneurs will make mistakes in their plan: about the business model, the capital requirement, the market or the competition. Putting together a plan that can withstand the scrutiny of a private-equity firm requires hard work. Many entrepreneurs are not accustomed to having their ideas tested through discussion and confrontation. That is what the private-equity professionals bring to the process.

When an entrepreneur comes with an idea that is basically sound but we have less than complete confidence in his or her ability to execute it with their present team, we try to attach other people to the venture. In fact, it has become one of the key roles of a private-equity firm to bring additional skills on board to improve the chances of success.

By far the most common addition is in the area of finance. We often have to assist the entrepreneur's understanding of the financial dimension and the role of the finance director.

Many young entrepreneurs could be more successful if they had a good financial executive on their team. Some do not really understand what an accountant or a finance director does. In some cases – for example where the entrepreneur is a former academic, engineer or scientist – he may not have had much exposure to these people before. Smart investors will insist that the appropriate financial skills are in place from the outset, because they understand that when you invest in an entrepreneurial venture, you are contending with both business risk and financial risk.

As a business grows it requires more working capital. It may be that your customers will finance your increased working capital by giving you longer credit terms, so instead of getting thirty days' credit you might get sixty days' credit or ninety days' credit for the supplies that you purchase. It may be that you can manage to get suppliers to provide you with consignment sales, for which you do not pay until you have sold them. It may be that you negotiate increased facilities with your bank.

Who on your team understands these dimensions? If you are expanding fast, you have to make appropriate provision to avoid the risk of running short of cash. Overtrading – meaning that the business is growing faster than its financial resources can sustain – is a real danger. Before you know it you have a potentially valuable business but you do not have the capital to support it. You do not have the cash to pay your suppliers or your employees. You run the danger of going bust.

Who on your team understands all this and has the expertise and the experience to prevent it?

It is easier to manage the finances of a large business than a small one, because you can attract financial talent to a large business relatively easily. For a small business it is much more difficult to do. Somebody who has the appropriate skills in the financial sphere might be working for a large company, and he might be there for reasons of job security. If you offer him a position in a small company, which has less job security, he or she may well turn it down. When you have achieved credibility in the marketplace it is much easier to attract financial talent.

Because it is difficult to recruit good finance officers to small businesses, we will often find there is a finance director who has not been tested, he has not been with the team for long and he does not know exactly what he is doing.

Sometimes we find that the financial controller or finance director is not a sufficient influence on the entrepreneur. In some cases, because the finance officers tend to protect the downside rather than look for the upside, they are not really respected by the visionary entrepreneur. If there is a meek finance director and a powerful, entrepreneurial chief executive officer, the finance director might not stand his ground and sufficiently challenge the entrepreneur's views. That can be dangerous too.

A finance director should have a forceful enough personality to get attention. We look for that quality in the early meetings.

In my conversations with my nephews about the Australian property venture, we talked about adding to the team. We discussed the type of finance director they needed. They could get an accountant who had worked in property but had no experience of working with banks. In my view, that would not have brought in the necessary skills. They did not need just the basic skills of accounting. It was not only about making sure the business's books were well kept. They also needed another skill, which was the skill to get on with the banks; to inspire their confidence and to obtain credit from them through the most appropriate financial structures and at the lowest cost.

Defining the objective of the company defines the kind of finance person you need.

At Apax, we would say to an entrepreneur, 'Don't just get your business model right, understand the financial model that you and your finance director are managing, and make sure that that financial model operates efficiently and within an acceptable band of uncertainty.'

One might find in certain circumstances that a retailer looks solely at the product line, buys too much stock, is unable to sell it and goes bust. It has happened a thousand times, especially in the fashion business. What does the finance director bring to that? What the finance director might bring to that – or what an entrepreneur who understands the financial dimension might bring to that – is a change in the system where you have to buy all of your stock months ahead of time.

One of Apax's investee companies, the fashion retailer New Look, realized: 'Our ability to predict demand is down to about six weeks. We want to be able to place an order now and to have it in the shops within six weeks.' All of a sudden, the business model changed completely. Their ability to react to changes in fashion was much greater and the financial risk they were running – because their inventory was reduced down to six weeks' worth of stock from three months' – was much lower. They reduced at the same time both the working capital of the business and the risk they were running. It made a huge difference to the prospects of New Look.

If the financial side is well provided for, the next issue is: 'Does this entrepreneur have a team around him or her that is capable of delivering the plan?' If it is a marketing-led business, do they have a first-class marketing manager? If it is technology-led, do they have a first-class head of research and development? Do they have a complete team or is it just an entrepreneur who has yet to build his team?

Professional investors would much rather deal with an entrepreneur who has already assembled a team that has made a proper contribution to preparing the business plan. If the team has been together for some time, it is a big plus. It is certainly much better than an entrepreneur who comes with a blue-sky idea and no team. From an investor's point of view, that entails the highest risk.

We used to struggle with the issue: if you have a great product and a great market opportunity but weak management do you go with it? We came to the conclusion that you were better off having a great manager with a slightly lesser opportunity, if only because the great manager will eventually gravitate towards the best opportunity.

If somebody comes to you – whether you are an investor or an entrepreneur – with a great idea, you have to ask, 'Do they have the execution skills?' If they do not, be careful.

I often used the phrase: we would rather back jockeys than horses. Ideas abound; the rare skill is effective execution.

Poor management can destroy a good opportunity.

Investors back jockeys, not horses

—

*

If the entrepreneur looks good, the opportunity seems real, the financial dimension has been addressed and the team is impressive, the investor then looks carefully at the business plan.

When you are a sole trader or a two-man or three-man partnership earning fees for services, you probably do not need a business plan, just an action plan.

But when you are expecting to have an organization, offices, overheads, products and services, customers and distribution networks, you must have a business plan.

The initial drafts of such a plan are really the reflection of a set of assumptions about the scale of the opportunity, the appeal of the product, the competence of the team and the strength or weakness of the competition. Such a plan tells you the performance you must deliver in order to achieve the desired results. It also tells you how much capital you will need to deliver that performance. But such a plan is not yet ready to be implemented. It has not yet been tested and found to be robust.

In order to get to a plan that has been thoroughly tested, you need inputs from different directions. Above all, you need to do due diligence.

Due diligence is the process of research and investigation by which you answer key questions. Are the sales projections realistic? Where is the market data and analysis to support those projections? Has the concept been subjected to market research? Have we anticipated how the competition will respond? What happens to our offer if the competition reduces its prices? Are our operating margins realistic? What benchmarks are being used to justify those projected margins? Are the costs of development, production and marketing realistic? Have they been tested? Has the necessary work been done on process engineering and design? What about the overheads? Are they in line with the projected increase in output? Is the forecast capital investment and working capital requirement realistic? Is the projected exit value, through a flotation or a sale, realistic? Is the projected timing of the exit realistic? Have we factored in possible exchange-rate fluctuations, interest-rate fluctuations and cost inflation? How much debt can the business access as it grows? How much additional equity capital will it need, and when?

Professional investors will push and pull the plan this way and that, looking at it from every angle and requiring you, the entrepreneur, to come up with convincing responses. At Apax, we would spend hundreds of person-hours on due diligence for every promising investment proposal we wanted to pursue. In that process, the numbers in the plan change, and sometimes the management team's desired skill-set changes also. Perhaps the sales forecasts are reduced, or spread over a longer period of time. Perhaps the pricing of the product is brought down in anticipation of the response of the competition. Product launch targets are often deferred. Whatever is done to the plan to make it consistent with the findings of due diligence, it will change the bottom line. And it will change the initial and subsequent capital requirements.

In the old days, an entrepreneur would come in with an idea and a sketch of the business plan. The venture capitalist would help him to draft the business plan in great detail. As the private-equity market expanded, a higher quality of entrepreneur, often with considerable experience in business, came to the fore and venture capitalists would begin to demand a proper business plan from the outset. If we, the venture capitalists, did not have a proper business plan on the table we no longer became involved in preparing it. We just felt, 'This entrepreneur has not succeeded in putting together a good plan, how is he going to be successful in building a major business?'

Today the private-equity industry in general will require people to have a proper business plan at the first meeting, backed by analysis and due diligence. We will call people who have worked with the entrepreneurs and managers in question, there will be reference checks on their strengths and weaknesses, and we will get a sense of how likely the team is to succeed. Looking at the business plan, we look not only at the level of realism and the robustness of the financial model, but at the competition and the circumstances influencing the market's growth and its profitability.

This would include a serious consideration of timing.

The investor will be looking for a certain speed of accomplishment. The contract between the entrepreneur and the investor will include reference to the general timing of the exit. In our contracts we say: 'We will invest so much for so much of the equity and the objective is to go public in about five years,' or whatever the target is.

We are not saying to the entrepreneur: 'We'll invest such and such, you do the best you can.' He needs to have clear targets: 'Sales will be X by the third year, Y by the fifth year, and we are going to go public at a valuation of Z in year seven.' Those expectations are there from the beginning in his business plan. You have to have clear objectives from the outset.

What are the factors that affect the speed with which you achieve your objectives? There are a multitude of them; all of them will be reflected in your business plan in some way. The first is the amount of capital that is available at the start. Generally, if you have $100 million to invest, you should be able to achieve your objectives more quickly than if you have only $20 million. But that assumes that $100 million can be invested wisely. In all businesses, there is a limit to the amount of initial capital that can be wisely invested.

Other factors include the rate of growth of the market and the underlying situation in the broader economy.

Another significant element concerns what is going on in the marketplace and among your competitors, and your ability to take advantage of it. There are some entrepreneurs, who could be described as money-makers, who know how to calibrate these things very precisely. When they see that it is going to take a little longer to achieve their objectives, they will adjust their plan. When they see an unexpected gap in the market, they put their foot down on the accelerator to take advantage of it. There are others who are like trains travelling at a fixed speed towards their final destination: they cannot adjust to circumstances along the way.

Most important, a plan has to have an exit in mind. The private-equity business has gone from backing people without having any idea of what the exit might be to defining the exit carefully at the time of making the investment. We expect that the business is going to be of strategic value to a certain type of buyer and that the buyer is going to be capable of paying a certain price if we manage to get to a certain level of profit. Either that, or the business is going to be right for flotation on the stock market.

There is a probability attached to each of these outcomes: you cannot be sure which one will happen. We might even go to an investment bank and ask: 'If we were to float this business four or five years from now with these figures achieved, what kind of value do you think we might attain?' We thereby refine our assessment of the profit that we, as the investor, and the entrepreneur and his team can respectively make out of the venture.

While we are doing that, the entrepreneur is asking himself, 'If I let go of so much of the equity, am I doing it at the right valuation? How much of the company am I left with? On these terms and with these forecasts, can this venture make my fortune? Would another private-equity firm leave me with more of the equity?' It is generally best for an entrepreneur to have three private-equity firms bid for his opportunity, if possible.

The entrepreneur often focuses primarily on operations. We focus on operations and the numbers. But testing the initial calculation, the financial analysis, is something we do together with the entre-preneur. The younger the business, the less likely the original budget is to be met; new budgets will be set on a yearly basis as the business progresses, by agreement between the management team and the venture investors.

Sometimes there is a conflict between the idea of creating a great company, to which the entrepreneur is wedded – he is in love with it to a degree – and monetizing the return at exit in the dispassionate way that outside investors require. It does not have to be a conflict, but sometimes it is. On the one hand, you want someone to be willing to die, so to speak, for his vision, and on the other hand you say to them, 'Five years down the track, once it has got going, we will want to sell our stake.'

That is the obligation that comes with raising money. If you go public, you have to deliver results every quarter or six months. If you raise private equity you have to be able to deliver an exit after a number of years.

Either way, if you are not able to commit to delivering what your prospective investors expect you will not get the capital.

If the investment can provide a successful exit it is because the business has been successful. It is therefore likely that the entrepreneur will continue with the business. The original investors leave, but the entrepreneur stays.

The entrepreneur of today is taken by the venture capitalist through all this thinking. Raising capital is an intensive and often exhausting experience. Any entrepreneur who goes through the process of raising money from private-equity professionals gains X-ray vision about his venture on the way and a clearer view of his company's potential.

Part of the entrepreneur's learning involves benchmarking.

We apply various ratios to the business plan: for example, operating margins as a proportion of turnover. These ratios are derived from experience in the sector concerned. It is rare for a supermarket concept to achieve profit margins of more than 5 per cent of sales. It is rare for the gross margin of a supermarket business to be more than 30 per cent or 35 per cent of sales. It is rare for a manufacturing business to be successful without a gross margin of more than 45 per cent of sales. The return on equity in a public company is about 15 per cent.

There are benchmarks we would know in most sectors, which can be found by reading stockbrokers' reports. Such benchmarking is crucially important in calibrating business opportunities and in strengthening a business plan.

When you are running a business you are trying to benchmark off your most effective competitor, not the average. The same should be true when you work up your business plan.

Every now and then someone comes along who overturns prevailing business models and sets a new benchmark. Michael Dell might have said: 'IBM has the PC, but I think it is possible to be a much lower-cost manufacturer. There is no need to have the same overheads. We are not going to have large sales forces, we are going to sell through the Internet and direct mail and advertising. We are

DUE DILIGENCE AT THE EARLY STAGE

Every plan needs to be tested: that was the lesson for private-equity firms investing in early-stage businesses. Those that did little due diligence ended up on the floor, perhaps finding out too late that their new products did not meet the needs of the market – unlike this lo-tech innovation, from the Apax Christmas card of 1995.

going to source components and assemble in the Far East. We are going to shorten our supply lines and we are going to carry less inventory. We are going to provide the same product or better at a much lower price. We are going to undercut and outsell IBM while generating better margins.' Someone who is able to establish new benchmarks in this way will set a new standard for competition in the sector. Everyone has to respond or they lose market share.

We look for that. When we analyse business plans and measure them against industry benchmarks we are alert to the possibility of changing the way the industry does business. Tim Waterstone did it, Michael Dell did it, James Dyson did it and, in the capital market, the private-equity industry did it. If you can change the benchmarks, you can enjoy a considerable period of competitive advantage before the rest of the industry catches up with you.

You may ask: 'Are you saying that as well as all the other attributes of vision, drive, determination, leadership and energy, I need all this financial and strategic sophistication?'

The answer, for your team if not for you personally, is yes. Your finance director should be capable of getting stockbrokers' reports and calculating the basic ratios. Business school teaches you a set of skills to think about these questions. If you have not been to business school, some of your executives need to bring these skills to your company. If it is an early-stage business in a new market sector it may be hard to know what these ratios should be. You have to define your benchmarks as you go.

But make no mistake, given the greater sophistication of sources of capital today, the entrepreneurial business plan has to be more sophisticated than it was twenty years ago. The corollary is that you can raise much larger amounts than you could ever have raised before.

*

The venture-capital business is always associated with the magic phrase 'internal rate of return', or IRR. Internal rate of return is a measure of profit. It is the compound rate of return achieved over the life of the investment. Private-equity investors expect to achieve a higher return than they would receive if they invested in quoted shares or bonds or from deposits in the bank, to compensate for the higher level of risk being taken.

You will have been told that venture capital companies will not talk to you unless your plan can deliver an attractive IRR in a reasonable time-frame. If you have a good idea but it is going to take ten years to get to your goal, the gain needs to be substantial. Otherwise, venture capitalists will not invest. A 25 per cent internal rate of return over five years has traditionally been the benchmark for private-equity funds. Higher-risk, early-stage opportunities need to show about twice that rate of return to be interesting, while a typical buy-out will need to show an internal rate of return of about 20 per cent in current market conditions.

The venture-capital industry tends to look at a five-year time-frame. It has been compressed to three years in good times and it has been extended to seven years in more difficult times. On average it hovers around a benchmark of five years. A business plan that does not show returns – or a measurable and substantial increase in value – until after the fifth year is not very appealing.

The last question to address is: 'Does it matter where the initial investment capital comes from?' In my view, it matters a great deal.

First of all, you can see from everything I have written here that launching a new venture is a complicated and demanding business. When you raise money, you want more than just the cash in the bank. You want the input of a great investor. You want to be subjected to the rigours of the business planning process. The greater the rigour in planning, the greater the chances of eventual success. Private equity has become expert in developing and funding businesses. It is an expert at such things as the length of the runway and attracting managerial talent. It can transform your chances of success.

Venture capitalists are also smart enough to know that sometimes they need smarter money than themselves. Sometimes, for example, the venture investor will identify the need to find strategic co-investors who bring specific sector expertise.

In 2004, Apax took a 40 per cent stake in Vueling, a low-cost, domestic airline in Spain. We thought there might be an opportunity for a low-cost airline in a large country with significant urban centres. But it was clearly a high-risk venture. It was a start-up with a large capital requirement. Low-cost airlines operate on thin margins, competition is fierce and there are regulatory issues, as well as issues surrounding the semi-protected status of 'national' airlines. The airline business is a special business and we felt the need for somebody who knew the intricacies of the field, someone who knew how to get an airline going. So we introduced some really smart money alongside us in the form of Dave Neeleman, chairman and chief executive of Jet Blue, a low-cost, domestic airline in the United States. Jet Blue, via an investment vehicle, took a 7 per cent stake.

Vueling went from strength to strength and the company went public on the Madrid Stock Exchange in December 2006. Our stake was valued at more than twice our investment. We did not sell out entirely, retaining 21 per cent, on which we made an even bigger return. Overall the investment delivered an internal rate of return of 114 per cent.

The second reason for raising the smartest money you can find is that the game has changed in the last thirty years. Thirty years ago it was very tough to raise money and you were grateful to raise it from any source. There was no particular branding that went with the money you raised. But as the venture-capital industry has become more professional and private-equity firms have divided into leaders and followers, so there has arisen an endorsement value from being backed by one of the more successful firms.

If you are backed by one of the leading private-equity firms and you subsequently need to raise more finance, you raise it much more easily. If you need an investment bank to take your company public and you have a first-rate private-equity firm backing you, the investment bank will be more likely to agree to do it. If you need to attract top management and the venture is not yet entirely proven, top management takes comfort from the fact that you have a good private-equity house backing you.

In this way, the reputation of the firm becomes a combination of the reputations of the investor and the entrepreneur.

Another business we backed in Spain was called eDreams, in which Apax funds and 3i co-invested. eDreams is an Internet-based travel agency and holiday company. It is run by super-smart people. You could not invest with a more impressive team: highly intelligent, deeply analytical, competent. But it is a difficult market and it proved to be tough going. The management had to raise additional equity more than once. The fact that they had Apax and 3i on the board gave them credibility, without which they might not have raised the needed capital. Eventually, we sold out, making a profit on our investment.

Another example is Calvin Klein. This was an interesting case of how smart money can see an opportunity that suits the strategic ambitions of a management team. Bruce Klatsky had run a company called Phillips Van Heusen (PVH) for many years. Based in New York, PVH is a shirt manufacturer. But PVH did not have a major brand and Bruce dreamed of buying one. Calvin Klein was up for sale and the two companies were in negotiation. PVH was a public company, but Bruce was told by his investment bankers that stock market conditions made it impossible for him to raise the money he needed on the stock exchange. So Bruce turned to us to see if we would put up the money. Would we invest in PVH if PVH were successful in clinching the purchase of Calvin Klein?

The whole point of the deal was that, if PVH could acquire a major brand like Calvin Klein, there was great potential to create value for the combined business. Van Heusen was profitable and Calvin Klein offered an opportunity for profit improvement. If you put them together the whole company would be more valuable than the two parts separately.

We relied on the management to handle the integration of the two businesses. Apax funds invested about $400 million. When we sold out after about three years we made three times our money. The company has continued to do well.

The PVH-Calvin Klein story illustrates how the private-equity industry is prepared to fund transactions that the stock market will not back.

As an entrepreneur, what you are looking for in your investor is a partner rather than simply a source of finance. It is not like going to the bank and asking for a loan. You are looking for a partner who can sit with you, help define the issues, take a place on the board, act as a sounding board and help strengthen the management team to make sure that the venture progresses strongly.

After we sold out of Calvin Klein, the management of Tommy Hilfiger came to us. Hilfiger's business in the United States was going downhill; it was losing market share and the European management team wanted to buy it and turn it round. We made an investment totalling just under $300 million, drawn from Apax funds in Europe and the United States. The buy-out effect that comes from a highly motivated team with a significant ownership stake, and the freedom to act, is now being felt. At the time of writing, the paper value of the Apax stake has more than doubled.

Another example of an investment in which smart money was all important to support the management in doing daring things was Yell, the British yellow pages company. We financed the buy-out of Yell in 2002. At that time it was the largest buy-out ever in Britain. What is unusual about Yell is that it operates in a regulated marketplace. The Office of Telecommunications, Oftel, sets the rates that Yell can charge for advertising in Britain.

We had earlier made a successful investment in Thompson Directories, which is a small competitor of Yell's. We had purchased Thompson from two other venture firms. Those firms had stayed in with us and together we had supported the expansion of the business before we sold it to Telecom Italia.

From the perspective of the management of Yell, we were smart money: we understood their sector. They came to us with the proposal that they should really expand beyond the regulated sphere of the UK. They wanted to acquire a major company in the United States, which is an unregulated market. They asked if we would support them, first in buying themselves out of British Telecom, which was then under pressure to realize assets in order to reduce its indebtedness, and second in undertaking a programme of acquisition in the United States.

We said yes. It turned out to be a great investment for us, and for Hicks Muse, our co-investors.

The management of Yell, led by John Condron, was superb. Having acquired the business, the first company John Condron wanted to buy was the Yellow Book; it would cost $660 million. We helped to finance the acquisition, which transformed Yell. They achieved the diversification of revenue they wanted. Partly on the back of that acquisition we were able to float the company on the London Stock Exchange in 2003, with an IPO value of more than £3.3 billion. In two years, we made more than $500 million profit on an investment of just under $500 million. Yell has continued to do well; it is now capitalized at just under £4.5 billion ($9 billion).

After we floated Yell, a whole string of yellow pages businesses were bought by private-equity firms all over the world. It set off a chain reaction.

Something similar happened in the satellite business. In 2003, Apax funds were involved in acquiring a company called Intelsat, which uses satellite for media distribution. In 2004, we were able to merge Intelsat with another player in the field, PanAmSat, to create a large and successful satellite business. We had already also bought into Inmarsat. On every ocean of the world, in every harbour, in every yacht marina, the boats are equipped with Inmarsat satellite telephones. They are even used by the military. We floated Inmarsat on the London Stock Exchange, and did well from both investments.

Similarly, together with Texas Pacific, we bought TIM Hellas, the Greek subsidiary of Telecom Italia, paying a high price for it. We then acquired Q, the number-four mobile telephony company in Greece – again, at what looked like a high price. We put the two together, which enabled the merged company substantially to improve its profitability and its market position. TIM Hellas was sold in February 2007 to Weather Investments SPA, a company led by the successful Egyptian telecoms entrepreneur, Naguib Sawiris, for about $3.4 billion, giving Apax a return of 4.4 times our money and an internal rate of return of nearly 280 per cent.

In the case of TIM Hellas and Intelsat, we were able to define winning strategies ahead of investing. With PVH, Calvin Klein, Yell and Tommy Hilfiger, we backed management to do something daring. In the case of Vueling, we brought in investors who were expert in the sector.

The growth of entrepreneurship and venture capital over the last three decades has changed the rules of the game dramatically. It is no longer the case that the typical entrepreneur has to persuade a sceptical bank manager to provide him or her with the capital to get started. These days there is a vast reservoir of investment capital looking for opportunities and a whole industry sector, private equity, which has accumulated the required expertise to make informed, entrepreneurial investment decisions.

The modern-day entrepreneur will face searching questions when he or she goes to a professional investor for capital. The process of interrogation, business planning and benchmarking is rigorous and can be exhausting. If the entrepreneur is able to persuade the professional investor that he or she has identified a great opportunity, attracted a great team, fashioned a great business model and will deliver a great product, the capital will be provided, but with strings attached. The professional investor imposes constraints. Significant capital expenditures and hirings will have to be approved, reporting requirements will be frequent and detailed, performance expectations will be high and the penalties for falling significantly short can be severe.

But the fact that much larger sums of capital are available than ever before and that the firms investing this capital are so expert gives today's entrepreneur huge advantages that did not exist when I started out thirty-five years ago. The truth is that, once he or she has overcome the hurdle of securing the support of venture-capital or private-equity investors, today's entrepreneur has a high expectation of achieving significant success.

Smart money brings more than cash alone. If you go to a friend or a bank, you might get the money, but you get nothing else. If you go to a leading private-equity investor, or to any other recognized professional investor, you will get endorsement, insight, connections and expertise as well as money – and this will bring you a greater probability of success. The investor is your key partner: his expertise, as much as his capital, can strengthen your hand.

If you cannot persuade an investor to support your plan, it may be that the plan itself is deficient. Rejection can itself be a service, forcing you to go back to the drawing board. Far better to remedy problems at the planning stage than after the venture has been launched.

The supply of capital is not endless. In fact, as I will discuss later, it can be argued that there is still insufficient capital for investment in early-stage ventures, especially in Europe. But there is far more capital available now than at any time in history. Likewise, the supply of valuable investment expertise is not limitless. There are good investment firms and less good investment firms. But an entrepreneur with a great idea should have no difficulty connecting with a great investor.

For the fact is that the pools of capital and investment expertise have become greater today than the pool of smart entrepreneurs. Entrepreneurs have become the rarer element. Take advantage of this. Put serious time and effort into planning your venture and presenting it well. The venture-capital investor is on the lookout for the entrepreneurial team that holds out a big vision for its business, as well as the promise of turning that vision into reality.

7

EGO, INTELLECT AND INTUITION

Ego is a turbo-charger, not a navigation system.

In my experience, there are three personal qualities that, separately or in combination, provide the drivers of every business decision: ego, intellect and intuition.

Deep down, most entrepreneurs are driven by the desire or need to make a mark. This driver is all about ego. Ego is not to be dismissed: probably it is the deepest source of entrepreneurial energy. As well as being powerful, however, ego can be destructive, especially if you allow ego to set your course. Ego should provide power, not direction.

There are two ways of looking at ego: as healthy self-esteem, which, in a business context, is positive; and as unhealthy egotism, which can be extremely damaging.

All ego needs gratification. But there is a difference between immediate gratification, which is what the self-regarding entrepreneur most craves, and the recognition that comes from long-term achievement.

For the entrepreneur, subjugating the need for immediate gratification, harnessing the ego and channelling its energy is an essential discipline for success, but this discipline is not always maintained.

In the early 1980s, I sat on the board of Sir Clive Sinclair's company, Sinclair Research. As I have described, Clive Sinclair was identifying market opportunities on the basis of his remarkable, imaginative grasp of the possible impacts of convergent technologies.

Identifying market opportunities was crucial for the hi-tech entrepreneurs of the 1980s and 1990s; so much so that the approach to funding hi-tech ventures shifted at that time from the traditional venture-capital approach – of backing jockeys not horses – to the view that if you found the right market opportunity and the right technical solution, management could then be brought in. The venture-capital industry moved away from the accepted concept of barriers to entry – mostly about the supply of capital and management – to saying that in hi-tech businesses the really significant barrier to entry is technological. Identifying the product or market opportunity and the revolutionary technical solution: that was the rarity. By comparison, raising capital and finding good management was easy.

This was the formula behind Google, eBay and Microsoft.

It was also the formula behind Sinclair Research. While Clive Sinclair had a brilliant understanding of technology and technological convergence, and had enjoyed success with his electronic calculators, computers and portable televisions, management was not his strength. When you look at hi-tech ventures, the people who had the vision were often technologists who could not manage. But those who went on to be successful were the ones who realized their shortcomings, brought in good management and allowed that management to get on with it. The ones who failed tried to do everything themselves.

Clive Sinclair tried to do everything himself. In addition, he insisted on the infallibility of his own personal reading of the market. He wanted to revolutionize the car industry with his diminutive C5 car. He thought he could do it because he believed he was the man who could revolutionize everything. He designed the C5 in secret, with little input from outside, and the car was a failure as a result.

Ego also let Clive Sinclair down in his relations with his investors. He believed that, in selling 10 per cent of his firm to outside investors, led by NM Rothschild, he had sold only 10 per cent of his independence. I pointed out to him that when you sell 10 per cent of your firm, you sell 100 per cent of your independence. What do I mean by that? If you have sold 10 per cent of your firm on the basis of certain agreed terms, you cannot take the money and then change the direction of the company. You cannot pour all your energy, against everybody's advice, into a car rather than a computer. You must stick to the plan investors backed, or else get their approval for change. In the event, we succeeded in keeping the C5 car out of Sinclair Research. But I and two other non-executive directors eventually resigned from Clive Sinclair's board because we felt that, despite his undoubted talent, it would be impossible for him to succeed.

In truth, in the early days of building up a business, the distinction between an entrepreneur's need for ego gratification and the needs of the company may be hard to discern. The entrepreneur has a small team, a great vision and boundless energy. He or she makes all the key decisions, the few employees are wholly beholden to him or her, and excitement and gratification are generated each time they put in place a building block of what is expected to become a great business.

In the early stages, the entrepreneur is, in a real sense, the business.

As the business grows, however, it has its own needs; these will eventually conflict with the desire of the entrepreneur for immediate ego-gratification.

I have come across some entrepreneurs – Bob Payton of the Chicago Pizza Pie Factory was one – who were visionary and charismatic entrepreneurs and natural money-makers, but not also great managers. They could bring a huge amount to the management team, but their leadership was not effective in delivering results from operations. The way they made decisions and the way they handled colleagues became an increasing issue as the business grew.

The best entrepreneurs are aware of the role they play relative to the needs of their business. They will sublimate their egos to achieve greater success. Other entrepreneurs will put their own interests ahead of the business, which will suffer as a result. These are usually the entrepreneurs who see themselves as the hub of the wheel, involved in and crucial to everything. Their companies do not generally grow beyond a certain size, unless they are lucky enough to have colleagues who are able to manage them.

How do we know when ego is in the driving seat? If it is someone else's ego, it is usually obvious: ego is clamorous and articulate, impatient and intolerant. It sets the pulse racing. But if the ego in question is our own, the truth is often apparent only in retrospect. Entrepreneurs with demanding egos are not likely to be among the most self-aware; nor are they likely to be the most realistic.

Ego can be an obstacle to an accurate microcosm of the world in your head. Most successful entrepreneurs have learned to adjust this microcosm according to the feedback they get from the marketplace. Somebody may believe that he can achieve a certain market-share over a certain period of time. It may be that the firm does not achieve it, so he realizes that he was unrealistic about how quickly consumers would adopt his product. He then adjusts his model; he does not persist in his error. Ego can obstruct the adjustment process. Ego can lead you to persist in trying to prove, as management guru Peter Drucker put it, that you are right and the market is wrong. Driven by ego, some people continue to hold unrealistic expectations and make slow progress as a result.

Indecent haste is another manifestation of ego. Ego can drive you to make the wrong decisions, to get the deal done at any cost, to brush aside the need for due diligence.

To harness ego, to keep it out of the driving seat, the entrepreneur must give priority to intellect and intuition.

Intellect is relatively easy to identify: the research, the analysis of the facts, and the reasoning are all there for everyone to evaluate. In terms of decision-making in business, intellect is the opposite of ego. It is about calm, rational analysis of the evidence before arriving at a decision. It is about bringing due diligence to bear on every judgement. The whole of this book is about the application of intellect to business.

Intellect positions the long-term interests of the business above short-term personal considerations.

What then is intuition? Malcolm Gladwell, in his book *Blink*, says that, if you have more than four or five factors to conjure with at any one time, your brain's processes will move much faster than your reason can follow. The conscious part of your brain is only contributing so much, the rest is derived from processes that appear to be beyond reason. We all know situations where we say, 'Yes, I want to go with this.' We do not draw a decision tree. We know in our stomach it is the right thing to do.

Where ego is loud and attention-seeking, intuition is mostly quiet. It does not command, it is reflective and calm, a voice like that of conscience. When things are going well, intuition has a kind of serenity. When things are going badly, it is unsettled and anxious.

If you wake up in the morning and you have misgivings – a sinking feeling in the pit of your stomach – you should go with that feeling, you should not ignore it. If it is trepidation, that is different, but if it is a feeling that you are about to make or have just made a mistake, then you should listen and rectify the mistake. You should follow your intuition. Why? Because intuition subsumes intellect. The more analytical work you have done, the more reliable will be your intuition. If you have done exhaustive due diligence, if you have years of experience, if you have been faced with similar decisions before and if you have seen the results of your previous actions, it is likely that you will be well-served by your intuition.

Harnessing the positive energy of the team's egos as well as your own, engaging their intellects and encouraging the use of their intuition, is all part of entrepreneurial leadership.

The entrepreneur's aptitude in this respect becomes clearly evident in decision-making. There are egotistical entrepreneurs who need to make all the decisions. Others see their role as the fulcrum of a scale on both sides of which are the views of their colleagues. They see their job as assessing the weight of opinion and going with the majority view. Yet others see a scale on one side of which they will throw their weight once they have heard the views of both sides.

In my experience the third approach is much the most effective. The exercise of judgement is not a democratic process, it is a leadership responsibility. It necessitates the expression of a collective view that does not bring the egos of the participants into play nor alienates those who are on the 'wrong' side of the outcome. It is crucially important to avoid building camps of egos ranged against each other, where some feel they have 'won' this decision but 'lost' that one.

At Apax, I achieved this collective view by stressing that some people are better at protecting the downside and others are better at assessing the upside. Relatively few are equally good at both. If you view it in that way and you realize that the views of every member of the team are valuable in getting to the right decision, and if you express the consensus in a way that is not divisive while reflecting the views expressed, people walk out of the room feeling satisfied. If they were in favour of the decision, they say, 'Well, we came out in the right place,' and, if they were against, they say, 'We have a successful history of making decisions in this way. I am happy I expressed my views because the decision is better as a result.'

At Apax, we never voted on any decision. Voting crystallizes the contention between egos. I assessed all the inputs from my team and worked out what in my experience was likely to be the best way to move our business forward. I was the final arbiter of a decision that we had arrived at together. Having listened to all points of view, I would summarize the discussion, focusing on the issue, never focusing on personalities, and reinforcing the feeling that our collective decision-making was the key to success.

In my experience, many entrepreneurs' egos prevent them from actually hearing what they are being told: they think they listen, but they do not take their colleagues' views into serious consideration. Every decision is theirs alone.

Harnessing your own ego and the egos of your team is not only about decision-making and leadership style. There is no doubt that, as the organization expands, its very growth makes important demands on the ego of the founding entrepreneur.

An entrepreneur who has been busy establishing his business, winning the next order and raising finance, finds that he has increasingly to balance his activity between externally facing issues and internally facing ones. More time is spent dealing with employees and internal processes. Few entrepreneurs enjoy this, not least because little ego satisfaction goes with it.

At some point, the entrepreneur may have to harness his or her ego and decide that he is no longer the best person to manage the company from day to day. With fast-growing companies, this can become the case at a relatively early stage. The founding entrepreneur might be the best at making decisions involving difficult judgements, but he might not be the best at leading their implementation. The time comes to appoint a chief executive officer (CEO). The entrepreneur might become chairman or he may keep the title CEO and appoint a chief operating officer (COO). Either way, he basically delegates to someone else the day-to-day management of the business.

Most entrepreneurs fear such a step.

In some cases, in technology companies for example, the founding entrepreneur may come early to the conclusion that his best role is to lead the technology dimension rather than to manage the business. There are plenty of examples of successful businesses where the original entrepreneur was a technologist who eventually went back to being chief technology officer (CTO). He might still be the largest shareholder in the company, but there is someone else who is the CEO.

If you are going to be a successful entrepreneur, it is important for you to have in mind a concept of the necessary evolution of your firm, and of your role within it. You will exercise all of your skills in building up the company, but you should know that, once you reach a certain size, you are going to have to attract talented, experienced people and delegate to them the management of significant parts of the operation. That does not mean that you cease to be the leader. Ian McGregor, the former chairman of British Steel, used to say: 'Where McGregor sits, that's the head of the table.' There was no doubt in his mind about who was the leader. An entrepreneur can maintain leader status as chairman or CTO because he is the founder, the visionary, without whom the firm would not have existed. But he must let go at a certain stage of day-to-day decision-making on some issues at least.

These issues are reflected not only in the tension between the needs of the company and the role of the founding entrepreneur, but in the stresses that can be felt in the company's hierarchy, as the egos of a highly entrepreneurial management team are harnessed.

In most firms, a hierarchy of opinion-formers emerges over time. No matter how large the organization becomes, you, as the leader, are of necessity going to pick a group of perhaps half a dozen who are going to be closer to you than others. You will not make major decisions without consulting them. By the time the company reaches a hundred people or so, this small group is often formally constituted as the executive committee.

Clearly, there is a danger that an ego-driven executive committee will alienate the rest of the team. It is therefore essential that senior managers learn to control their own egos, and that you ensure that membership of the executive committee is not denied to outstanding performers or important centres of the organization. This is often a delicate issue. On the one hand, the inner core may be the founding team that has been together for a long time and is bound by an invaluable level of trust. On the other hand, the company has grown, new people have been recruited or promoted from within, and the founding team cannot expect to guide the company forever. The solution to this is seldom to expand the executive committee in order to satisfy everybody's ego.

The way I dealt with this problem was to shift from a fixed hierarchy to variable geometry. We had an original core group of six people; the business had expanded internationally; there was a need to represent the international offices on the executive committee; two or three of the original group had to make way. But I wanted to keep everyone in the loop. If you do not have variable geometry, where the roles and status of the various senior managers change according to circumstances and need, you will have a major problem.

Variable geometry allows you to move senior managers off the executive committee to different positions without loss of status. If the company is moving forwards, there are always new tasks to perform, new challenges to meet. The trick is to say to a colleague whom you believe should step down from the executive committee, 'We need different representation on the executive committee' – you explain the problem as it is – 'and I do not think that the same six of us can stay on as we have done in the past. Three have got to change. I would like you to focus your attention on expansion to other countries' – or a particular aspect of the investment process, or heading a particular committee, or taking responsibility for a specific part of the investment approval process. 'We will continue to keep you informed and we will invite your input on specific issues, but other people do have to come in.'

The answer is, therefore, that you expand the size of the senior group, but they are not all members of the executive committee. The number of people around the table has to be kept at five or six. The others will be able to make inputs, you will discuss strategic issues with them, but when it comes to operating decisions you cannot hope to get twelve people around the table each time. With twelve people, the decision will invariably be the wrong one, because it will be too conservative.

Occasionally, you come across people who resist joining the executive committee because they only want to get on with leading their part of the business. They do not want to become involved in the direction of the firm as a whole. Most of the time that is easy to accommodate. But some of the time their reluctance to get involved is driven by ego. In fact, they really believe that they should be the CEO, that they should be leading it all. They do not want to be in a subaltern position. That, of course, makes life more complicated.

In most cases, such a person will leave to set up in business on their own, or to go to a more senior position elsewhere. So be it. Identify them early and make plans for their replacement. Better still, if they are a really valuable member of the team, find them a position within the firm where they can make more decisions and take more responsibility. Give them an avenue to personal fulfilment that is in step with the needs of the business.

Finding the balance between ego, intellect and intuition is especially important when it comes to recruitment. A team comprised entirely of rampaging egos would not function well for long. Equally, a submissive team in awe of the founder will not achieve anything outstanding.

Some entrepreneurs find it extremely threatening to recruit able people. They subconsciously want to stay as the hub of the wheel, to control all decisions, because their ego demands it. They must have gratification every day, and this is best guaranteed by the overt exercise of power. They transmit that message to all potential

THE SECOND BOUNCE OF THE BALL

recruits, and, of course, the best applicants realize that they will not be listened to, let alone empowered, and so decide against joining. If an entrepreneur has an excessive ego, it is difficult for him to recruit people capable of independent action. His potential as a leader is limited.

In my experience, women tend to be more intuitive than men. Because I believe that intuition plays a crucial role in business, I have always tried to recruit women. We have had some outstanding female executives at Apax. The truth, however, is that women are either not attracted to, or are not as well accommodated within, the world of business as men. There are many great women managers, such as Marjorie Scardino of Pearson or Rose Marie Bravo of Burberry, but there are still too few women entrepreneurs.

Oprah Winfrey is one. In fact, she was recently voted the 'most admired' entrepreneur in an American poll. Starting in radio as a teenager, she was a news anchor at the age of nineteen. She moved into television, where *The Oprah Winfrey Show* became a phenomenon: the highest-ranked television show in American history. Winfrey used this platform to launch her own media production company, Harpo Inc. (Oprah spelled backwards), which now employs more than 250 people in television production, magazine publishing and online media. She also founded the Oxygen Network, a cable network for women. She has her own lifestyle magazine, *O – The Oprah Magazine*, and a thriving lifestyle website, *Oprah.com*. She has, in effect, turned herself into a major brand.

Another example is British cosmetics manufacturer and retailer, Dame Anita Roddick, founder of the Body Shop. Whereas Oprah Winfrey describes herself as an accidental entrepreneur, Anita Roddick followed the classic trajectory of entrepreneurial success, starting with an insight into a market opportunity and building a great business from scratch. Born to Italian immigrant parents, Roddick first ran a café in Brighton, on the south coast of England. She once said that the café taught her the basics of enterprise. She had the idea for making and selling eco-friendly cosmetics, but when she wanted to open the first Body Shop no bank would lend her the money. They would, however, lend it to her husband. Six months later, needing capital to open a second store, she sold 50 per cent of the business to a private investor. Thereafter, the company's expansion was funded from its own revenues. In 1984, just eight years after its launch, the Body Shop went public. It has since expanded to become a major, worldwide retail brand, with 31,000 employees and stores in 55 countries. The company was sold to L'Oréal in 2006 for about £650 million.

These role models, however, are very much the exception. Whatever the reason, the relative scarcity of female entrepreneurs is to be regretted. The world of business is the worse for it.

One area where it is possible to attract outstanding women – not necessarily drawn from the world of business – is to non-executive roles on company boards. A well-constituted board can assist in balancing the inputs of ego, intellect and intuition at the strategic level.

Most entrepreneurs are most comfortable with an executive committee they lead. It is only when they raise finance from outside investors, or make the transition to becoming a public company, that they have to deal with a board of directors. When the business reaches that stage, you will find that you need a board (including powerful non-executives) run by a chairman, while the company is run by the CEO through the executive committee. The chairman and the CEO are then two different people. The board is responsible for strategy and for the appointment of the CEO, for the approval of budgets, mergers and acquisitions, and other strategic decisions. The CEO's job is to implement the board's strategic decisions and to manage the day-to-day affairs of the company.

At this point, matters can become fraught. The ego of the entrepreneur can be an obstacle. Sometimes, the clash of egos between entrepreneur and non-executive chairman (or, if the entrepreneur has opted to take the chairmanship and to appoint a CEO, between the entrepreneur and the CEO) can be a serious issue.

Whether the entrepreneur remains CEO and reports to a chairman, or moves up to being chairman and hands over management responsibility to a CEO, depends on the role the entrepreneur wants to play, which is often dependent on the age at which he or she achieved success. Assuming that the entrepreneur has not reached retirement age, he will generally continue to be the CEO and he will look for a chairman who is both a figurehead and a sounding board.

If you have raised capital from outside the company, your non-executives might include representatives of the investors. Their role is to defend the shareholder interest, which, you hope, will not be in conflict with your own interest or with the long-term interest of the business.

Corporate governance can, of course, generate its own tensions; there have been many boardroom conflicts driven by contending egos.

At Apax, I did not have this problem. Apax is a partnership; we did not have a board of directors. Instead, we recruited a board of advisers. These were, one could say, candid friends who had no agenda other than to be helpful and constructively critical.

Three in particular worked extremely closely with me. One was Sir John Nott, who had been consecutively a merchant banker at Warburg, Secretary of State for Defence at the time of the Falklands

War and then chairman of Lazard. He was an Apax adviser for a decade. The second was Sir William Barlow, who had been head of a number of large organizations, including the Post Office. Bill was a very wise counsellor. The third was Sir Harry Solomon, who had built up Hillsdown Holdings into the largest food company in Europe, employing 55,000 people, and who is now my fellow founder and trustee in The Portland Trust, about which I shall say more later.

I found the counsel of these wise men invaluable. They had experience of large organizations and were particularly well connected. Each could empathize with a growing business that had great potential. I could discuss with them issues related to building the firm as well as issues with the portfolio.

Eventually, your company reaches the stage where you have achieved much of what you had dreamed of when you started out. Paradoxically perhaps, not all entrepreneurs find their fulfilment as the firm reaches this long-sought-after status. If your gratification comes from being the clear leader making all the decisions, and from the feedback you get every day – the confirmation that only you are in charge – then you will find the adjustment as the company grows difficult. If you have a better balance between meeting your own needs and making an effort to satisfy the needs of the business, you will adapt more easily; you will view the adaptation as part of the challenge of growing your business. Even so, you may not be enjoying yourself as much as you were in the early days when it was just you, a few colleagues and your dreams.

By the end of my tenure at Apax, I was spending more time on management issues than I wanted, despite the fact that we had appointed leaders of five sector teams who were managing their own people. We had an investment committee, an operating committee, an exit committee: different groups of people who were sharing management responsibility. Like every successful firm, as we grew we spent more time on the process of getting decisions accepted and implemented internally. For an entrepreneur, that is not necessarily a fulfilling development. More and more time is taken up with people issues, remuneration issues and internal follow-through.

Had I not delegated to senior managers, the situation would have been intolerable for me and counter-productive for the firm. Just as it was hugely liberating for me in the early stages of the business to become independent of my partners and free to run the British operation as I saw fit, so, in the later stages, delegation to senior colleagues came as a great relief. I could focus on driving the company forward without having to deal with every management detail.

If you let your ego get in the way of that process, your business will suffer. The extent of your success will be limited by the extent of your personal reach. If your competitors are not so constrained, they will do better than you.

At the end of the day, the greatest gratification comes from building the largest, most successful company. The pay-off is the satisfaction that comes from realizing your original vision. That is more likely to be achieved if you harness your ego, apply your intellect and develop your intuition – and lead your colleagues to do the same.

8

CHANCE, PERSEVERANCE AND LUCK

Luck is seldom
just a matter of chance.

People say that you have to be lucky to succeed. Of course, we can all benefit from good luck, and we can all feel dogged by bad luck. But I believe that in most cases, and in the long run, luck – in the sense of pure chance – is not a deciding factor.

In 1975, when MMG seemed in danger of falling apart and the four partners were at loggerheads, we agreed that we would each write a paper setting out how we saw the prospects for the firm. My partners followed the standard procedure of extrapolating from past performance to arrive at a set of financial forecasts. Each produced somewhat different numbers, but two were agreed in their conclusion: the venture, they said, was doomed.

For my part, I wrote a paper on the relationship between perseverance and so-called luck. What my paper said was that if we gave up and ran for cover, we would have lost a good opportunity. If we persevered we might find an unexpected client or come across a very successful investment. In my view, extrapolating the future based on the past told us nothing. We had to have confidence that, if we persevered, we would get the breaks and we would be successful. The key was to persevere. As actor and muscleman Johnny Weissmuller said when he was asked how he felt about playing Tarzan in the movies, 'The most important thing is not to let go of the rope!'

My two pessimistic partners were not persuaded. They chose not to persevere. But, sure enough, we did get an unexpected client, Lawry's Foods. At the same time, I was able to turn MMG's problems into an opportunity by identifying and attracting Alan Patricof into a partnership with me, initially in corporate finance and subsequently in venture capital.

Was I lucky? Yes. Was my luck the result of chance? No. It was immediate proof of my proposition that perseverance is the key to being lucky. The two partners who left the firm missed out on a great opportunity.

A well-known story is that, in 1980, Microsoft's Bill Gates referred IBM, which was looking for an operating system for its new personal computer, to a company called Digital Research Inc (DRI). DRI had developed an operating system called CP/M. But IBM and DRI failed to reach agreement. When he heard this, Gates offered to supply the operating system himself. He went to a company that made a system similar to CP/M, and became their exclusive licensing agent. Microsoft adapted the system and delivered it to IBM as PC-DOS. Microsoft subsequently licensed versions of this system (labelled MS-DOS) to the makers of IBM clones. The rest is history.

Bill Gates was in a position to take advantage of an opportunity that arose seemingly by chance. The founder of DRI, Gary Kildall, did not perhaps appreciate that he held a large part of the future of personal computing in his hands. Indeed, Gates himself has reportedly professed never to have understood why DRI failed to reach agreement with IBM. Whatever the truth, Microsoft emerged with a winning hand, while DRI came away with nothing.

Was Gates lucky? Yes, in that DRI had an opportunity to do a deal with IBM and failed to take it. Was his luck the result of chance? Not really. Gates spotted the opportunity, understood its true dimension and put himself in a position to take advantage of it.

Good luck arises from putting yourself in the best position to take advantage of events. As often as not, bad luck is evidence that you are on the wrong track.

In the case of Bill Gates, the chance to deliver an operating system to IBM turned out to be exceptionally significant, even decisive. It is likely, however, that Bill Gates and Microsoft would have been successful in any event. They would have got there by one route or another. Why? Because they made every effort to help themselves, knowing that every now and then, circumstance would help them as well. If it had not been IBM, it would have been something else.

The first rule of luck is that you should persevere in doing the right thing. Opportunities will come your way if you do.

Entertainment entrepreneur Haim Saban provides another example. He had gone through a challenging time as a television and video product salesman. He was in Japan when, by chance, he saw *Power Rangers* on television. He realized immediately that the programme would have international appeal and he bought the worldwide rights to it. He knew how to market it. He sold it to broadcasters all over the world and it became a television sensation. The success of *Power Rangers* enabled Saban to build his business and then merge with a division of Twentieth Century Fox to create Fox Kids. In 2001, he sold out to Walt Disney for $5.3 billion. The deal made him a rich man.

You could say that Haim Saban was lucky to be in Japan and to see *Power Rangers* when he did, before someone else bought it. But many of his competitors were not as assiduous in their travels as Saban. They were not in Japan. Those who were, did not see in *Power Rangers* what he was able to see in it. The fact that he was in the right place at the right time was a matter of perseverance, not luck. Haim Saban was an ambitious entrepreneur who was in search of a product that would have mass appeal. He wanted to break away from being a mere salesman of other people's products. He came to the conclusion that he had to own or control the rights to something big. He was constantly on the lookout. He found what he wanted in *Power Rangers*.

Perseverance is only the first element in the luck equation. The second is networking. I would say that luck is directly proportional to the size and appropriateness of your network. For many years, I was out several evenings a week with clients and contacts. I intuitively understood that such networking was an important part of doing the job. The more active you are, the more opportunities will come your way. The more people you know in your sector, the more often you will encounter circumstances that help your cause – an effect that is sometimes known as synchronicity.

A good example of synchronicity occurred just before I left Apax, when I set myself the mission of finding a head for our New York office. I had the idea that it would be useful to visit the people on the East Coast who were investing in my competitors, and to find out from them if there was anyone in private equity who was planning to move to another firm or to strike out on his own. I went to the offices of one of our investors. Sure enough, I bumped into someone I knew who had become a leading figure in a small private-equity firm. He happened to be in the offices at the same time. We had a chat in the corridor, and soon enough he was head of our New York office. I can give umpteen examples of that kind of synchronicity. It may look like pure coincidence, but it only happens if you are active in building and using your networks and knowing as many people as possible in your field.

I recently wanted to start a new business in real estate, because I think real estate is an asset class due for transformation. I thought, 'Whom could I recruit?' I came up with the name of someone who is a terrific expert in real estate. I called him up and asked him if he would join me. He said, 'I'll be there.' He had just been thinking of giving in his resignation at the place he was working. Coincidence? Yes. Luck? Not entirely.

When you are young and trying to launch your venture, you do not have a network. You have to build it. My friends could never understand why, in the early days of Apax, I would take a plane and travel all the way to Los Angeles in order to have one interesting meeting. For me it was obvious. If you meet interesting people who do clever things, something valuable comes out of it – maybe not today, maybe not tomorrow, but one day. You need a critical mass of such people. It puts you in position to spot opportunities, spot good people and spot new ways of doing things.

When you start out, especially with a new product or new market opportunity, you are not very visible in your field. Few people know you. You have an idea of what you want to become, but you cannot really know what is going to happen when you first enter the mar-ketplace. You cannot be certain, for example, when and how the competition will react. Once you get started, you discover that growth is not linear. Early-stage investing is famed for being a

J-curve. You make losses for a period, then you come back up to the break-even line before heading into growth. When you are above the line, into the upper part of the J, it is not going to be linear there either. Things happen in fits and starts. It may take you a few years to get your product right. It will take time to get established in the marketplace and then to achieve meaningful scale. But in the process you are becoming increasingly visible, and, as your visibility increases, other people start networking with you. In other words, once you become established, your network grows without you having to make all the running. It becomes easier to be lucky.

Building a network not only brings you connections that might lead to getting business, but also information about what is going on. At the same time, it puts you in a position to create relationships with people with whom you can interact subsequently.

As you climb up the experience curve, you will learn an increasing amount about your field. After three or four years, you will find that you have a much better ability to calibrate, to judge, to make decisions and also to become lucky. If you go into the property business you will know a good site from a bad one, a good tenant from a bad one, a good real estate agent from a bad one, a good source of finance from a bad one. You gain an understanding about the nuances and complexities of your market. You find that events are subject to multiple causation and that perceptions are coloured in shades of grey. It is not that this option is great and that option is terrible. The world does not tend to offer uncomplicated choices. The world delivers opportunities that are a blend of good and bad. You have to be able to calibrate, or assess, them. Your ability to measure problems and opportunities accurately improves as your knowledge of your business and of your field matures. You are improving your chances of getting lucky. You become more expert at dealing with situations that seem too uncertain to those in your field who are less well informed.

What you find is that you are able to make a decision between the best possible opportunity in theory and the best opportunity possible in practice. Many people, when they start out, are looking for the best possible opportunity. But they have no experience on which to base their judgement. With experience, you realize that business is not about the best possible opportunity but about the best opportunity possible.

You must put yourself in a position to benefit from events and circumstances more than your competitors, to become 'luckier' than them by understanding the business more deeply than them and grasping better than they do the opportunities that present themselves.

In investment it is essential to balance risk and reward; to compare this opportunity, in terms of uncertainty and financial return, with other opportunities you have seen before. Is this expensive relative to the past? Is it expensive relative to other opportunities now? Experience is your guide.

Look at the buy-outs financed by the private-equity industry in the three years up to August 2007. There is no doubt that, as a multiple of earnings, the industry was paying more for buy-outs than ever before. More debt was used in acquiring businesses than previously – partly because, until very recently, debt finance was plentiful and interest rates low. In general, private-equity investors were taking a higher level of financial risk than before: paying more and taking on more debt. At the same time, competition across the industry meant that rates of return were under pressure. Later-stage investment performance has been more predictable, it has attracted vastly more capital than was the case when I first entered that market in 1989, entry prices have gone up, and returns have correspondingly been reduced.

Then you ask: 'Where are we in the economic cycle? Is the outlook rosy or is it vulnerable?' The answer today is that the outlook is vulnerable. Why? Because there is still a huge credit balloon, interest rates have risen and the use of investment derivatives obscures capital market forces while amplifying them, consumer spending is coming down, and there is a high level of geopolitical uncertainty. Against that background is it wise to be doing more expensive and more leveraged transactions? Should we be putting money into buy-outs of mature businesses or can we find growth opportunities – perhaps including start-ups or early-stage investments in new areas such as new energy sources – which provide a better balance between uncertainty and returns? Do they give us a better chance to get lucky?

At Apax, four or five years ago, we had a senior member of our team looking at alternative energy. It was clearly going to be a major sector, but nobody in European private-equity had focused on the technology. The uncertainty was perceived to be high and the valuations were low. Result? We made nearly thirty times our money on the $11 million investment in Q-Cell: a $300 million gain in under three years.

I call this a matter of calibration; you are far better able to calibrate opportunities that present themselves to you when you are up and running, and your business is moving forward, than you were at the start.

You learn from your business as it grows and changes. You deepen your understanding of the marketplace. You get to know your competitors and how you can get ahead of them. You put yourself in a position to be 'luckier' than them.

Twenty-five years ago in private equity, being 'lucky' meant realizing that early-stage tech investment by itself would not be a success in Europe in the way it had been in the United States. It would certainly not be as successful as buy-outs. It meant understanding that sector specialization would be essential. It meant understanding that management skills and the added value they could bring to opportunities would be decisive. It meant understanding that, as both business models and investor interest became more global, the private-equity industry would move from establishing national funds to regional funds, and then from regional funds to global funds, and that the size of private-equity funds would increase greatly, increasing the scope to do larger transactions within each fund.

Learning from my own business, and understanding these things, meant that I could take advantage of circumstances and be 'luckier' than most of my competitors.

Networking and learning from your own experience are thus the second and third elements, after perseverance, in helping your own luck. The fourth is being flexible enough to respond quickly to changes in the market.

You must live and breathe the strategy of your business, trying to push it forward in a direction that will give you the ultimate prize of leader of the sector.

At Apax, it took us from 1972 until 1981 to raise our first £10 million fund. By the time we had $1 billion under management in 1996, we were established through many international offices as a developing global player. That meant never standing still, never being satisfied, always being on the move, and being flexible about our capacity, our geographical reach, the types of funds we raised and the sectors in which we were active.

Getting into the buy-out business in 1989 was crucial, even if the fund we raised for that purpose was our least successful. This fund actually targeted 'buy-ins' – which were buy-outs of under-performing companies requiring an immediate injection of management – but no sooner had we invested the money than the business cycle began to turn. It became our worst performing fund. But it took us into buy-outs, a completely different and important area of private equity with very high growth potential.

A dramatic example of flexibility on a large scale is Nokia. As I mentioned before, Nokia, a long-established Finnish firm, was making rubber boots and cables. They had a strong market position but the business was going nowhere. It was like making buggy whips. No matter how good they were, the market was in decline. How many rubber boots could they sell? Insulated cables was a mature market. They were fully aware of the problems, and initially tried to diversify by making televisions and personal computers. Neither venture was a success. Then CEO Jorma Ollila saw an opportunity in a new market, mobile telecommunications. He must have reasoned that it was somewhat related to Nokia's telephone cable and computer businesses. In fact it was a departure that involved significant uncertainty. Ollila used the financial base of the existing business to move into a completely new sector, becoming in the process the world's largest manufacturer of mobile phones.

He was right. In fact, the market grew so fast that Nokia ran into logistical difficulties in the mid-1990s. This led to a restructuring of the business and much greater emphasis on logistics and delivery.

You do not change the skills of the management team and the entire direction of the company without strong vision and strong leadership. Ollila is now widely credited with transforming Nokia, which had been riven by internal faction-fighting in the 1980s, into one of the world's most successful high-technology companies.

The mobile-phone business still has significant growth in prospect, especially in India and China, but Ollila's successor, Olli-Pekka Kallasvuo, is already talking about turning Nokia into an Internet company. 'Staying put,' he is reported to have said, 'is not a possibility.' At Nokia, they have turned flexibility into both a strategic principle and a culture.

Two questions arise from this. The first is: what element of flexibility is built into your plan? The second is: if it is a start-up or early-stage venture, to what extent should you expect to revise the plan within a relatively short time-frame?

First, it is not unusual for companies to be behind plan. Most early-stage ventures are behind plan in the early years; they might overtake the plan later if they are successful. An element of contingency, in terms of the timing and funding requirements of the plan, is therefore built in at the outset. Secondly, the greater the degree of uncertainty, the higher the level of adaptability required. You know that things are not going to turn out exactly as expected and you keep an eye on the plan at all times. It could be that it will need to be revised fairly soon after you introduce your product to the market.

Among the qualities I look for in an entrepreneur are adaptability and flexibility: an ability to respond to circumstances. I look for an entrepreneur who has strong analytical skills. And I look for the plan itself to allow for a degree of realignment and revision. Large capital projects, like building the Channel Tunnel, do not have much scope for flexibility, except possibly in the funding arrangements. Technology ventures often have considerable in-built flexibility: if one application does not work, there could be another.

You are working for the short-term and the long-term at the same time. That is an important concept. You are not only dealing with the short-term; thinking that the short-term will lead to the long-term. It does not work like that. You have to work for the short-term and the long-term at the same time. Microsoft's rivals thought that Bill Gates got a lucky break with IBM. But Bill Gates did what DRI failed to do. At the outset, Microsoft did not even have an operating system to offer. Gates realigned the company to take advantage of the opportunity.

Flexibility, improvising as you go along, perhaps having to change direction: this is what it takes to win. You push at doors to see which ones open.

The fifth element in helping your own luck might seem to contradict the notion of flexibility. This is the need to stay focused on the right opportunity. But, as any successful strategist will confirm, there is no contradiction between strategic focus and flexibility, just as there is no contradiction between maximizing your upside and protecting your downside.

As you grow, so your expertise grows, your network grows and it becomes easier to be lucky. But there comes a point at which growth raises the question of diversification: should you keep all your eggs in one basket or should you have several different baskets – that is to say, should you develop several different product lines.

There are innumerable examples of a technology that has five different applications. Most entrepreneurs will try to go after all five, on the basis that they are giving themselves a better chance of success. Technology ventures have a high level of uncertainty; where there are high levels of uncertainty it seems natural, even prudent, to hedge your bets by backing several different products at once. Your product is going to take time to develop.

You think, 'I'm competing with the largest technology companies in the world and they may beat me to it. I cannot just bet the whole shop on a single product. Why don't I have five different products in development? Then I know that I have got at least one chance in five of coming through.'

The problem is that a small team cannot cope with five opportunities. If you are chasing after five opportunities your probability of scoring a hit is not one in five, but very much less, simply because you are dividing your efforts in respect of any one product by a factor of five times. You end up with five underdeveloped products, one going to the consumer market, one going to the corporate market, one with this aspect, one with that aspect: the result is that your people and resources are split and your business cannot be effective.

There are optimum levels of diversification and focus. Unless you achieve focus you are not going to win, for the simple reason that in each of those five markets there are competitors who are going to be more focused than you are and just as intent on succeeding.

Even large companies can lack focus. IBM felt so threatened by the Apple II that they rushed their PC into the marketplace. They used off-the-shelf hardware components, a non-proprietary operating system and non-proprietary software, for which all the clone-PC manufacturers – Dell, Compaq and the rest – were grateful. (They could never have cloned the Apple with all its proprietary features.) Strategically unfocused, IBM created a market that others were better able to exploit and which it eventually had to leave.

You have to define the main chance and focus on it. You should also define an alternative in case the main chance does not come through. Eliminate all the other possibilities. If you are building a business you must establish yourself in the marketplace. If you do not have sufficient focus, you will fail.

Sometimes the desire to chase after five opportunities reflects the personality of an entrepreneur who has a great idea today, who is

"NO YOU CAN'T MAKE ANOTHER ONE 'TIL YOU
FIND A USE FOR THIS ONE!"

Many an opportunity has been missed for want of imagination in supporting further R&D investment. This 1998 Apax Christmas card expressed the idea well.

going to have another great idea tomorrow and who will have another even better idea the day after. None of them will be followed through.

More often seeking five opportunities rather than one or two is the result of the fear of a concentrated bet. I think that, even for a logical person, the chances of success might appear so small that it seems wiser to hedge his bets, not realizing that he is reducing his chances of success, not increasing them. There are plenty of instances in the Apax investment portfolio where we have said, 'You know what, these three other developments are quite interesting, but they are not going to do much for the company, and they will absorb time and resources. Let's just put them on ice for the moment and concentrate on one or two core opportunities.'

Psychologically, it can be difficult to close down a line of research or product development. It is like chopping off a limb. But it has to be done.

At Apax, as I have described, we moved from early-stage investment to buy-outs. We moved from being UK-focused to being regional and then global. We built up expertise in high-growth sectors early and steered clear of other sectors. Overall, we certainly stayed focused on our market; although, had we gone into hedge funds in 2000, we might have been successful in entering a wider market, that of alternative investments.

I have already noted the apparent tension between strategic focus and flexibility. There is another apparent tension: between concentrating on the home market and taking advantage of international opportunities. Businesses increasingly have to be international almost from the word go. In earlier times you would build a national base and only later would you consider international expansion. But now there are so many business models that require you to be international from the outset, either because you want to avoid being copied internationally or because there are synergies to be gained from being in a number of different markets. If you are in investment management, for example, it is imperative to have a presence in the United States. If you postpone getting into that market you might later fall behind your American competitors.

Much modern-day business is international: capital is international, component supply is sourced internationally, some services are now contracted internationally, the markets are international and the competition is international. Even in a quite modest business, production might be subcontracted internationally.

The international dimension thus applies today to most businesses. I first became conscious of the importance of this in the early 1980s, when we backed a small British computer company called Future Computers. Future Computers was trying to do what Dell did in the end: to design cheap but high-quality IBM-compatible products. But Future Computers quickly discovered that if they were going to be successful they needed to have engineers and clients in the United States. This little company, based in South London, had to open an office in San Francisco in order to stay close to developments in Silicon Valley.

They then discovered, as Dell discovered, that they could not manufacture in the United States or in Europe at acceptably low prices, so they had to open another international office, this time in the Far East. So this tiny firm had an office in Croydon, an office in Taiwan and an office in San Francisco. Needless to say, they were not successful. Their skills were the skills of a small, London-based company. Although they had the ambition to be a global company, they were relatively inexperienced in business and were based in Britain, where the electronics industry was less vibrant than it was in the United States. They were trying to do this at the same time that much better-financed American businesses – which were attracting executives from IBM and other established companies – were doing the same thing.

We realized even in the mid-1980s that certain business models required an international footprint, and that they posed the challenge of attracting international management skills very early on. Such skills were much harder to find than those required for a national business.

The international aspect has changed in recent years with the Internet, the spread of PCs and telecommunications improvements. There is now an ability to manage an international business in a way that was never possible before. Size of firm and international reach no longer increase together. There are in fact few purely national business models today. For one thing, in Europe, with the creation of the European Union and the Euro-zone, you have basically one market with one currency. Very few European entrepreneurs today want to capture only the Italian market, or the Spanish market, or the French market, for a particular product. Most firms will think of selling across several geographical markets within the EU.

When you are talking about expanding internationally and opening facilities in different countries, the challenge varies according to the sector. Generally, it is easiest to do in services and more difficult in manufacturing. It is most difficult in retailing, as the British retail giant Marks and Spencer found when it tried to open shops in France. The difficulty of assessing locations and understanding consumers, and of managing challenging logistics, has made it difficult for retailers to expand into foreign markets. There are few examples of successful international retail chains.

Another factor militating against international enterprises is the difficulty of assessing people of different cultures, and the related difficulty of integrating different national cultures within one corporate ethos. At Apax we operated in eight countries and we deliberately internationalized each office. We did not have all the British in Britain, all the Germans in Germany, all the Italians in Italy and so on. In order to cross these cultural bridges we put people of different cultures in each office and got them used to working together, so that across the firm we could begin to have a common language. The typical national attitudes of, say, Germans when confronted with one situation, or of Britons, needed to be mixed together so that you developed a common language and a common set of values. The handling of teams across all these different nations was a challenge that needed to be met.

For a Briton, say, to assess a German or a Swede in an interview requires experience. In some countries understatement runs much deeper than in others. Hyperbole in Spain or in Italy is equivalent to understatement in Sweden. Even with experience, it can be hard to understand the nuances of one culture compared with another. It was partly for this reason that Apax's joint venture in Japan failed.

It is going to get easier, of course. People get educated across borders today. A significant proportion of people at Apax went to international business schools. They came from all over the world, but business school gave them a common language, common concepts and common values.

Even if most businesses these days have an international dimension, however, that does not mean that they should not maintain a strong focus on their domestic market. On the contrary, I think that huge advantages derive from being successful in your home market. The larger the home market, the better – not only because it gives you a substantial base on which to build, but because you get used to levels of competition that are much higher than in smaller markets. It is not an accident that American designer jeans cost more in Britain than they do in the United States. The price umbrellas that have been established by the manufacturers in Britain have been established in environments where there is less competition than the United States. If you are used to the cut-throat competition in America, you are in a good position to take advantage of less competitive environments internationally. Despite the fact that Americans are regularly characterized as having no understanding of other cultures, they have been by far the most successful at international expansion. Look at how many multinationals are American-led. They are in the majority.

International expansion can involve high risks. There are many entrepreneurs who feel they should develop internationally before they have established themselves on a solid footing in their national market – meaning that the business is competitive and profitable and its growth prospects are assured. My advice to those entrepreneurs is: 'Do not get distracted by trying to open up in the United States or in Germany. Establish your firm in your home market, create a great management team, create an efficient engine, and then go.' The fear of somebody else getting there before you, while sometimes justified, may lead you to over-extend yourself from a management point of view, and you will do less well than you should in your home market.

You should take calculated risks, not bet the shop.

The rest-room-door advertising entrepreneurs whom I mentioned earlier came to me a couple of years later and told me that they had made good progress in Britain and they had been approached by a third party about opening up in the United States. They wondered whether they should seize the opportunity. I asked them about the prospects for growth in Britain and they told me that the prospects were good, that there was still a long way to go. When I asked them if they were managing the business satisfactorily, they said they needed to bring in some new people to strengthen their management team.

My advice to them was to get properly established in Britain and to make sure the new people were bedded down before diverting their attention to the United States. I knew that America would absorb a huge amount of time, they might get it wrong, and they would not have the flexibility to stay there long enough to correct it. They did not have a large enough base in their home market. If it started going wrong in the United States they would have to withdraw to protect their business in Britain.

They followed my advice and focused on growth in the UK. They have since expanded their British operation to include poster advertising in service stations and they have launched a creative-solutions division for promotions and sampling.

A successful entrepreneur develops a sense of the probability of success attaching to certain moves. What is the level of uncertainty in the decision and what is the probability of getting it right? If you have pay-offs that are substantial with a high probability of success in your home market and you are still a small business, it makes sense to take advantage of those before you move to more difficult opportunities internationally.

This is a principle I would apply to building your business in all respects, not only in terms of international expansion. It particularly applies in the international area because the effort involved in an international step is geometrically greater than a similar effort nationally. If you are in London and you want to expand to Hull, Manchester or Liverpool, it is much easier than trying to expand to Paris, Berlin or San Francisco. Of course there are exceptions, and the exceptions, as always, are as important as the rules. But the challenge involved in establishing something internationally is much greater than in growing something organically in one place.

The sixth, and final, element in helping your own luck – after perseverance, networking, learning from your own business, flexibility and focus – may well be the most important; it concerns leadership and involves turning every apparent setback to your advantage.

As your business grows, so it changes. It is constantly evolving and you are always having to adjust your offer to the market – in response to competition, technological change and other opportunities or threats that present themselves. From time to time change will be harshly imposed on you. A competitor might come up with a product or service that is much more threatening than you could have envisaged.

One of your important resources might walk out of the door: a key partner or key technology officer might leave, perhaps to join a competitor. You need to rise to the challenge every time that happens.

It is not a question of just coping with that event; it is a question of turning it to your advantage. This is not only a matter of saving face, of cosmetically glossing a step backward so that it looks like a step forward. Rather, it is a fundamental precept of entrepreneurial leadership.

As your business changes, so you have to reshape it and redirect it. But such reshaping and redirection can be hard to achieve. In most businesses, internal change, no matter how necessary, is difficult to bring about. This applies especially to personnel. If you have a trusted band of people and you think you should let one of them go, not because he or she is not performing at their best but perhaps because

The secret of lucky entrepreneurs is the will to turn every setback to advantage

you need someone who is more qualified to take the company to the next stage, you probably will not do it. You are loyal to the person you have, even if by keeping them you are probably doing them no favours in the long run. As the business outgrows them they will become stressed and unhappy, and will under-perform. Even if you let the thought of letting them go cross your mind, you probably fear a negative impact upon the group as a whole. So you do nothing, and the business suffers.

The leadership of an organization is constantly being judged by the people in it. Every event in a company, internal or external, is the occasion for judgement. Your staff will be aware that their colleague is holding them back. They look to you to solve the problem. Turn the situation to your advantage: let the person go and get someone better.

Supposing a good person leaves of their own accord? Even if you had not realized that you needed to get somebody better, it would be an opportunity for you to trade up, to get somebody who can take you that much further forward. An apparent setback thus provides an opportunity. Setbacks enable you to make changes that otherwise you might have shied away from making. This is an important technique in building a business and it is an important factor in so-called luck. A good executive leaves; the way to prove you are moving forwards despite his departure is to focus the firm on bringing in somebody of a higher calibre. The new person will enable the firm to achieve goals that could not previously have been contemplated.

Using change to your advantage in this way is partly about being clear-sighted and analytical. Many people are more emotional than analytical; if someone good leaves, they see it as a catastrophe. They think they are unlucky, and they allow themselves to become so.

Of course, if the number two is brilliant and the number two leaves, that is a real blow to the leadership of a business. For the leadership to recover from that blow might involve realizing that the executive in question ran his particular division extremely well, but what is now needed is somebody who has much deeper skills in, say, the technology area. Replace the departing number two not with a new manager of his division, but with somebody who is a technology leader. In that way you will raise your game.

Some reinforcement of the role of the leader should take place every time there is a challenge to the organization.

What is it that allows you to turn apparent setbacks into opportunities? The underlying concept is that at certain stages in the development of your organization you can recruit people of only a certain level of ability. You may get lucky and a star stays with you all the way, but mostly it is not like that. If a person should leave for some reason and the organization has moved on since they joined, then there is a strong likelihood that you can recruit someone of higher ability to replace them. In other words, growth provides opportunities to recruit at a higher level. Growth provides the conditions for being lucky.

Fundamental to turning an apparent setback to advantage is the exercise of will. People can get dejected by what they perceive to be a setback. The will to view it as an opportunity and to get the organization to view it as an opportunity is essential if you are to hold the team together.

Napoleon famously required his generals to be lucky above all else. But as Napoleon knew well, a great general does not depend on luck. He anticipates the rain, he takes into account the 'lucky' downpour that might trap his enemy in the mud.

Entrepreneurs are also required to be lucky. Invest in building your network. Remember that as you grow, you will become more visible. Eventually, people will start networking with you. Make it a principle of your leadership to see all change, even change that is forced upon you, as an opportunity to push the business forward. Turn everything to your advantage. Be flexible, study your own business, and be prepared to make adjustments as you go along. Do not dissipate your effort across numerous opportunities: focus on your core business and your core market. Only diversify into new products and expand into new markets when you have a solid base on which to build.

If you do all these things and persevere, trust me, you will be 'lucky'.

9

DOING IT RIGHT

Principles have a cost,
but they are always
a bargain in the end.

This book is primarily about entrepreneurial leadership; no discussion of leadership would be complete without due consideration of moral values.

When I talk here about moral values, I am talking about principles that can be dictated by considerations that are moral as well as prudential – that is, in terms of the benefits they can bring according to what is generally known as enlightened self-interest.

The fact is that it takes wisdom to build a great company. Wisdom leads eventually to fulfilment, which is ultimately about achieving a healthy balance between what you do for yourself and what you do for others. Of all the observations I have made in this book, this is the one of which I am the most certain.

Apax could only grow to the size it did in my time because we had an agreed set of values: personal and corporate integrity; meritocracy; maintaining long-term relationships based on trust, internally and externally, with our investors and the entrepreneurs we backed; leadership; and stewardship of the firm by each generation in turn. Our business practices were always governed by the highest ethical standards. These standards were not only an informal code, they were an integral part of our internal policy guidelines and they were enshrined in our mission statement, which hung on the wall of the reception area in each of our offices. They were reinforced over the years as the firm grew and changed. In April 2000, by which time we had a large, complex corporate structure, offices in a number of countries and a host of different nationalities among the staff, I addressed the company on exactly this topic. I said that while it became ever more certain that we could build Apax into the leader of our sector, so it became ever more important to articulate our values and to apply them uncompromisingly, so that anyone who did not share and observe them should leave the firm.

Apax only grew to the size it did because it strived to be a good place to work and to treat people well; because we pursued ethical investment policies; and because we treated our stakeholders – the companies and entrepreneurs in whom we invested, our investors and business partners, and the local, regional, national and international communities of which we were a part – with care and responsibility.

Just as, when I set out, I had the ambition to build a great company knowing that personal financial rewards would surely follow, so my partners and I built the firm on the basis of strong ethical principles, knowing that in the long run, and all else being equal, corporate success would follow.

We were right. In fact, the ethical approach has a great track

Fulfilment lies in reaching a balance between what you do for yourself and what you do for others

record. Among the longest-lived and most successful companies in Europe are those, such as Unilever, which have a tradition of ethical conduct, not least towards their own staff.

Others, for example those firms founded and run by Quakers, have combined long-term success in business enterprise with forward-thinking social commitment. My own model was McKinsey. I knew from my experience of working there that it operated to the highest ethical standards, convinced that there really was no other way. McKinsey's values were those I adopted for Apax.

This aspect of corporate behaviour is all too often overlooked. Hollywood and the media prefer to paint corporate life in the colours of greed, hypocrisy and moral laxity. Such stories are inevitably more colourful and, since they always end with the bad guys getting their just desserts, they are more morally exemplary than everyday stories of decency, hard work, technological innovation, wealth creation and the improvement of the lot of the common man. When one looks at recent cases such as Enron, Arthur Andersen, WorldCom and Tyco, one can only admit that Hollywood and the media have a point.

But the real lesson to be learned from, say, Enron is that its senior executives were destined to be found out from the moment they abandoned the ethical path. Whether it was in respect of their insider dealing, their misleading accounting, their illegal trading practices or their misrepresentation of the company's prospects to staff and stockholders, the truth about Enron could not be suppressed forever. Sooner or later, it would emerge into the light.

Contrary to their own estimation of themselves, the Enron executives were not the smartest guys in the room. While it seems that, among the senior executives and the traders, each pursued the shortest path to personal riches, they ignored the rule that, for the corporation as a whole, sustained success depended upon wise, and that means ethical, leadership. In 2000, Enron reported gross revenues of $111 billion and its stock stood at $90. Then the scandal broke and within a year the company filed for bankruptcy. More than 20,000 employees lost their jobs and saw about $3 billion evaporate from their pension funds.

The demise of Enron took with it the entire global operations of the company's auditor, Arthur Andersen, which at the time was one of the world's Big-Five audit firms. In direct contravention of the ethics of the accountancy profession as well as the law, Andersen executives shredded Enron files rather than disclose them to investigators. It was as good as signing the firm's death warrant.

As the biblical Book of Proverbs says: 'A good name is more to be desired than silver and gold.' Reputation is everything. When Andersen shredded the Enron documents, it shredded its own reputation. The firm, which had been founded in 1913, and which for decades had been a byword for probity, was hounded by investigators; in 2002 it voluntarily surrendered its licences to practise as a chartered public accountant. Overnight, 28,000 jobs were lost in the United States and 85,000 worldwide.

We have seen several examples of profiteering, rigging of markets and the abuse of political connections by corporations in recent years. But I do not believe that the firms engaging in such practices can thrive in the long term. Why? The fact is that it is much harder to maintain a web of deceit and malpractice than it is to operate above board successfully. Regulatory systems are designed to catch thieves and prohibit sharp practice. On a commercial level, if you behave badly, your suppliers and customers stop doing business with you.

Business logic also demands that, at the end of the day, the books must balance. If you are booking future sales as present income, as Enron did, you are going to find it increasingly difficult to balance the books.

Even were none of this true, even if it were possible to spin out a web of deceit for a long time, the fact is that your company will fail in the end for the simple reason that a corporation that does bad things will get a bad reputation, and a corporation with a bad reputation will not attract good people or good clients.

Business history is littered with the corpses of companies that behaved unethically and paid the price.

Many companies have a moral as well as a prudential attitude towards behaving well, but sometimes fail to live up to their own precepts. Hewlett-Packard was once well known for its ethical standards and outstanding corporate governance and citizenship. It was recently overtaken by scandal, when, following the ousting of high-profile CEO Carly Fiorina, it was revealed that illegal investigative methods had been used to trace the source of leaks from the boardroom. Hewlett-Packard chairman, Patricia Dunn, was asked to stand down and was subsequently charged on counts of fraud and conspiracy. Actually, what the boardroom scuffle at Hewlett-Packard shows is not that the company was founded on hypocrisy but quite the opposite: that it had strayed from its own high standards and it knew it. It put in place the measures needed to restore its reputation.

The same was true for the scandal over allegedly rigged stock options that engulfed Apple: these things were put right precisely because these companies know the importance of reputation, inside the company as well as out.

My approach at Apax was always to be a hundred miles from the borderline of what is acceptable. I was not interested in investing in businesses that I did not think would reflect well on the firm. On one occasion, there was an investment opportunity that involved financing old people in their homes, so that they could, in effect, live off their capital. When they died, the business recovered the home, making a profit if the person did not live longer than the actuarial prediction. You could make money on it, but I was not interested in that. On another occasion, there was a debt-collection business. I was not interested in that either. I was not interested in armaments, gambling or any other opportunity that did not reflect well on the firm. I felt that there were enough decent opportunities without chasing after ones that had even a hint of being ethically questionable. Similarly, I was never interested in hostile bids, I was only interested in agreed bids and on being on the side of management – helping management to build better and larger businesses.

Doing it right at Apax meant adherence to five precepts. First, my word is my bond: if we agreed to something orally, it could be relied upon. Second, honour the spirit as well as the letter of agreements: we did not look to satisfy legal wording rather than the agreed intention. Third, full disclosure: for Apax, inadequate disclosure is lying by omission. It was always our practice to inform relevant parties in a timely manner of any information to which they were entitled. If a fund had a problem, we would tell the investors. If an indebted company encountered difficulties, we would tell the bank. If the firm had an issue, I would tell my partners. I certainly would not like a partner to find out from someone else what they should have heard from me. Fourth, act fairly: I stand up for myself and my firm and I will always insist on what is fair from my point of view. By the same token, I try to ensure that it is also fair from the point of view of the other person. This applies especially where there is an imbalance of power, for example between employer and employee. Finally, act responsibly: if you have power and authority, with it goes responsibility. I tried to ensure, for example, that I never put people into situations where they were vulnerable.

I think you derive great strength from adherence to principles that the organization – meaning its people at all levels – values and admires. Such an organization will attract and keep a higher calibre of individual. The best people flock to the corporations that, from an ethical as well as a commercial standpoint, are doing great things. People want to feel passionate about their jobs, their careers and their personal integrity. They want to be recognized and admired. For them, the objective of the organization is not only to be financially successful but, in the long term, to earn a great reputation of which they can be proud. That dictates a certain type of behaviour, which attracts a certain type of person, which attracts a certain type of banker and a certain type of investor.

Some entrepreneurs mistake expediency – cutting corners, underpaying staff, inflating sales, habitual late payment of bills and so on – for good, aggressive business practice. Firms that behave in that way generally either stay small or are short-lived. You can only be the best if you attract the best people; you only attract the best people if you offer them a great vision; and a great vision includes great ethics.

Today, I would go further: I would say that to attract the best people you need both a moral dimension and a social conscience. I will deal with this more fully in the next chapter, where I discuss social enterprise. For the present, I will note that when I interview prospective employees today, they are interested in our social mission. The best candidates are not content to be only for themselves, or to delay until their retirement doing something that is good for others.

Look at what is happening now in business schools everywhere: corporate social responsibility and social enterprise are among the most popular courses. People have a feeling that there is something wrong with successful, entrepreneurial society. As it gets richer, the gap between the haves and the have-nots seems to grow. The haves benefit from great wealth and great profits. The have-nots increasingly occupy a parallel world of unchanging disadvantage. In other words, even if no one is actually or knowingly behaving badly, even if every corporation adheres to high ethical standards, the market system itself can lead to unacceptable social outcomes. Even if you do not regard this as morally wrong – which I do – prudence would tell you that, if those who are successful do not put something back in to help those who are being left behind, society is going to explode violently. The market does not take care of all its social consequences.

Social mission is becoming a leading aspect of our age's business culture. It is increasingly a part of how successful entrepreneurs conduct themselves in the world. We have seen two of the world's richest individuals, Bill Gates and Warren Buffett, donate a large part of their respective personal fortunes to a foundation for medical research, and for other worthwhile causes that could benefit, they believe, from a hands-on, entrepreneurial approach. Rather than pay a share of this capital in tax, and depend on government to tackle these problems, Gates and Buffett are donating 100 per cent and tackling the problems themselves, using the private-sector approaches that have proved so successful for them.

There will always be people round the table, of course, who are interested in nothing more than immediate personal or corporate profit, even if there might be a risk to the firm's reputation. They want to cut corners or they want to back a questionable business. They begin to rationalize the opportunity in a way that makes it as palatable as possible from an ethical point of view. The deal is marginal, or possibly even damaging, in terms of its reputational return, and they have to rationalize it somehow. That can be the start of a slippery slope. If the ethical principles of the business are not set out clearly, it can be hard to know where the borderline of acceptable behaviour lies. Soon enough there is a blurred or flexible border. Executives overstep it without knowing, and before long the reputation of the business suffers. The impact is felt within the organization and on the bottom line.

Part of the reason for Apax's success was that investors knew they could trust us to do the right thing. We were not going to embarrass them. Some of our competitors were as trusted as we were, but there were many others that were not so trusted; they have not thrived. In the private-equity industry, you must earn and keep the trust of your investors in order to thrive.

I was once involved in a transaction in which Apax was the buyer of a company, and where the seller, despite the fact that there was an exclusivity agreement (during which we had the opportunity to conduct detailed due diligence of the company and the seller was forbidden to entertain offers from other parties), decided over the weekend to do a deal with one of our competitors. I found out at the last minute and I telephoned the vendor's CEO, with whom I was vaguely acquainted, and said: 'You are morally committed to this agreement and as far as I am concerned you are also legally committed. It is just not right that you should do this. You should do the deal with us at the agreed price, or, at the very least, you should give us the opportunity to match the price you are now being offered.' He replied, 'I don't know that I can do that.' I said, 'Well, that will be a great disappointment to my firm and we will have to consider what we do about it.' He did the deal with the other party and I put lawyers on the case. In the end, he paid us $15 million in compensation for all the work we had done, and for breaking his word.

We received the $15 million, but a number of banks, law firms and accounting firms had done work for us on a contingent basis. We could have kept the $15 million, but it did not feel fair. Instead we kept half and distributed the other half to those who had worked on the transaction with us. I sent substantial cheques to the investment banks, the commercial bank, the lawyers and others, saying, 'It did not work out, but we have successfully got compensation from the vendor and we think you deserve a share of this given the considerable work you have done.' We felt a moral obligation towards them; it was not fair that we should keep it all.

Sometimes there are tough decisions to be made that impact beyond the firm. The domestic appliance manufacturer Dyson was based in the small town of Malmesbury in Wiltshire, 100 miles west of London. James Dyson was the largest single employer in the town and it appears that he was very socially engaged. His reputation was that of a good employer and the firm was held to be a model of corporate citizenship. However, for a manufacturing business to be based in Britain was tough. The cost base was too high. In the end he had to move. He moved the whole operation to the Far East. From a business point of view it appears to have been an essential move. If he had not taken that decision, the business would have declined and the impact on the town would have been negative in the long run. But he did make that decision and the negative effect on Malmesbury was immediate.

For me this is a clear-cut issue: you have to do what is right for the business. Your own self-interest and the interests of other constituencies must come second. The existence of the business is the prerequisite for it to play any positive social role and its existence will be in danger if the leader does not do what is right for its success.

The same rule applies to the founding entrepreneur. Some people hang on to leadership long after it has ceased to be in the interest of the business. And they know it. They will admit it. But they say, 'So what? This is my business, I built it and I do not care if somebody else could do it better. I am going to continue until it suits me to leave.' When you think in that way you are making a wrong business decision. It might be right for you personally, but it is wrong on every other count and the business will inevitably suffer.

Ideally, a healthy enterprise culture – in the context of a functioning and fair democracy that attends to the interests of all its citizens – will create appropriate jobs in appropriate locations for appropriately trained and remunerated workforces. The responsibility of the entrepreneur is towards his business, expecting either other businesses to take advantage of circumstances that no longer work for him or for workforces to respond to changing circumstances by retraining or relocating. Of course, there can be significant short-term stresses created by this approach, but such stresses are preferable to the long-term decline that leaves post-industrial wastelands and multi-generation deprivation, such as are seen in some impoverished towns in Britain. Putting constituency interests ahead of enterprise results in failure, both for business and for the community.

In fact, Dyson found that, partly thanks to the reduction of his production costs, the company was growing at such a pace that his research and development operation, which stayed in Malmesbury, was taking on more and more people. Within two or three years his total employment in Malmesbury was actually higher than it had been before, comprising a high added-value skilled workforce much more suited to Britain's relatively high cost base.

In dealing with such issues, it is crucial to convey your values to your firm and to your wider constituency before you get to a situation where there might be conflict. Being a good communicator really helps. Some have it, some do not. In terms of management styles, there are good communicators who may not be good managers, and good managers who may not be good communicators. But good communication and the power to persuade are terrific advantages, especially if you want your business to communicate certain principles that are different from those of your competitors.

If you behave properly and fairly, it marks you out as a different kind of company. You create an image for the firm of being a cut above the rest. You may make a little less money in the short term, but you create an organization that everybody can be proud of and that others want to do business with. In the long term you will be more successful.

This is the same lesson that I applied in giving that first cheque to Alan Patricof. If you can act according to principles, rather than in terms of your financial interest, you build bonds of trust and a sense of obligation.

Trust and fairness are crucial ingredients in the life of a business. This rule applies internally as well as externally. Of course, there are dysfunctional or disaffected people in every organization, but I believe that the great majority of people who worked for Apax would say that they could trust that the firm – whether in the matter of salaries, bonuses or some other aspect of day-to-day working life – would always settle matters fairly.

On an operational level, any entrepreneurial organization, if it is going to function effectively, ends up functioning on trust. You cannot have extensive command and control mechanisms. You are delegating to people and you are counting on them to go as far as is reasonable to go and no further. The great advantage of a system of this kind is that the people to whom you delegate feel empowered. Empowerment means that they are more fulfilled by the achievement of what they do and are much more motivated to achieve difficult objectives. In order for this feeling of trust to result in an organization that does not go beyond the bounds of what is defined as being acceptable, you need a strong culture of responsibility to do the right thing for the firm. It is a culture that draws clear lines of demarcation between behaviour that is acceptable and behaviour that is not. You empower people by trust and you create in them a reciprocal sense of obligation.

From my observation, the dog-eat-dog culture is not a successful one, even if there are occasional exceptions to that rule. Such a culture leads to the predominance of individual interest over the interest of the firm, to the detriment of the firm.

If you trust people and they trust you, you can achieve much more. Potentially difficult tasks are easier to manage. For example, you create values in your organization that are designed to create a sense of forward momentum and continuity. You do not create an unstable environment where people fear that they could get to the office one day and find that their desk has been cleared and they are out of a job. If you create a sense of security and fairness and good order, then you will encourage loyalty to the firm and you will get the full benefit of people's talents.

From time to time there will be people in the firm who cannot keep up with the business. That is just how it is. Some people refuse or are unable to adjust to new realities and, in some cases, they have to leave. You might have a loyal finance director who was fine in the early years, but the business has expanded so much that you have moved from having an accounting-driven finance function to a function that is dealing with banks and investors and with the raising of capital and complex compliance issues. It can be difficult to turn the accounting-driven finance director into this new type of finance director. You may have to effect a separation.

In that case, it is crucially important to deal fairly with the person leaving, in order to set a satisfactory precedent, so that everyone in the firm can see that the matter has been well handled, and for others, who might be in the same position one day, to know that the firm will be fair. The person must be dealt with in a measured way; they must be remunerated handsomely for the contribution they have made, and given assistance in finding a new position elsewhere. You might also find that the separation will be a relief for them.

The organization then judges that this is something that needed to happen in the interests of the business, that it has been properly handled, and that the person has been treated with respect and generosity.

Having people leave the firm on good terms is very important. In your business career, you can do good deals and bad deals; you can make money and you can lose money; but you only have one reputation and you must take every opportunity to consolidate it. If you deal properly with those who have served you well in the past but can no longer perform in the role that new circumstances require, it creates a sense of fairness within the organization. I have always asked myself one question in my dealings with people, whether they be employees, partners, clients or others: 'Is it fair?'

The exercise of fairness on a consistent and regular basis creates a sense of dependability. When, as inevitably happens, people who are unhappy within the organization blame the leadership for their unhappiness, the bulk of the organization will confront them and say: 'This organization would not behave in that way, you are wrong.'

The only problem with doing the right thing is that there is usually a cost in the short-term. The pay-off is in the long-term. When you cut corners it is the other way round: the pay-off is immediate, the cost will follow. When someone is leaving the firm, you treat them well. There is a short-term cost. The benefit comes when you recruit people in the future: you attract the best because they have faith that they will be treated properly. At the same time, you ensure the continuity of your team, because they too feel that they will all be treated properly.

Principles, whatever their cost, are a bargain in the long run. That is something I fervently believe in. It dictated how we behaved at Apax. People should never feel anything other than that the organization and its leadership are of the highest integrity.

This is not only an issue for the leadership: everyone in the firm must subscribe to the same standards. Integrity is absolutely crucial. Some people feel it as a moral principle, others feel it as a prudential principle. But those who do not feel it at all are the wrong people to have in your organization.

In the end, you want to be able to look at yourself in the mirror and feel proud.

10

EXITS AND ENTRANCES

Succession is a process, not an event.

One of the first realizations to dawn on the emerging private-equity industry some twenty years ago was that you needed to prepare your exit at the time you made your investment. In the early years, we would invest in a business – often a start-up or early-stage company with high growth prospects – without thinking too carefully about the exit. We tended to concentrate on the prospects for success, reasoning that, if the investment worked, the rewards would be significant. There was really no need to push the numbers for a flotation or a sale, or to assess the prospects for either in detail. The exit from a successful business would look after itself.

In those days, we had a better chance of investing at below market-rate valuations because the market for companies was inefficient; this provided a cushion of comfort when it came to the exit. Today you cannot buy substantial companies below market valuations: every buy-out goes through an auction. Adding value and understanding the nature of the exit has therefore become crucial. As the industry has invested ever-larger amounts of money, and has become increasingly concerned about delivering timely returns to its investors, it has become obvious that we need – at the point of entry – to have a view about the timing and value of the exit. Investors in private-equity funds are no longer content to hear talk about blue skies; they need a time-frame and they need forecast realizations.

In order to understand the prospective exit, we have to work out whether the business is more likely to be acquired by a trade buyer or whether we will be able to take it public. If we invest in a substantial buy-out like Yell, Britain's leading yellow pages company, we look for a stock market flotation. If we invest in Thompson Directories, a much smaller competitor, we look for a trade sale.

Every company has an exit scenario. As I described in chapter six, we work towards that exit from day one. We will ensure that we meet certain milestones – the launching of a product, the securing of a major order, the acquisition of a target company, the achievement of a projected financial performance – and at the appropriate stage we will call in an investment bank to help us prepare for a sale or to go public. Since the idea was to take Yell public, we immediately brought in a non-executive chairman and two non-executive directors to prepare the company for flotation. If we know that one of our investee companies is going to make acquisitions in the United States, we will bring somebody on to its board who has experience of acquisitions in America.

Since the boom period of 1995 to 2001, when Apax achieved fifty-two successful flotations on public exchanges, the early-stage IPO market has been slow and the private-equity industry has grown mainly on the back of buy-outs. Some of our investee companies, like Inmarsat, Azimut, Vueling, Q-Cell and Yell, have gone public. Others, like Thompson Directories and TIM Hellas, have gone to corporate acquirers. Yet others, like Deutsche Kabel and eDreams, have gone to other private-equity buyers.

As private-equity investors, we make our money on exit, not before. At Apax we used to say 'well done' to our people when they made an investment. We reserved 'congratulations' for when they made a successful exit.

In our investment contract with the entrepreneur all this is broadly mapped out. The contract might say, for example, that we envisage taking the company public after about five years and, if we do not, we should have a chance to sell our shares privately.

Virgin Radio was a case in point. We entered into a joint venture with Richard Branson. The agreement was that we intended to take the company public, but if he did not want to take it public he would have to buy us out at the valuation that the public market would have placed on the company. In the event, Branson did not want to go public, so we went to an investment bank and asked them to put a price on our stake and he bought us out at that price. All of this was spelled out in the original agreement.

Just like the private-equity investor, the entrepreneur has to think about the exit from the beginning. Certainly, if you plan to raise venture capital in any form you will be made to think about it. It is unavoidable. This is one reason for the much greater sophistication of business plans today.

If you want to build a lifestyle business, which you keep forever at a modest size and pass on to your children, do not bother approaching private equity. Professional investors will not be interested. If that is what you want, raise money from the bank or from family and friends.

The ambitious entrepreneur may have a trade sale in mind, or even a reverse takeover of a larger corporation, so that growth can be maintained and the business can go to a higher level.

Alternatively, you may want to float your company on the stock market. For many entrepreneurs, going public is a rite of passage. If, at the point of the flotation, the venture capitalist sells his shares at a decent profit and the entrepreneur and his team can take a little money out of the business while riding on the future with the rest of their shareholdings, it is a good outcome for both entrepreneur and investor.

To go public, however, there has to be an appropriate stock market. This poses no great difficulty for established companies, but an important area in which Europe has failed its enterprise community relative to the United States is in providing appropriate stock markets for early-stage ventures. So acute is this deficiency that a hi-tech entrepreneur wanting to start out in Europe today would have to think seriously about whether he or she might not be better off relocating to the United States, where there is likely to be a more receptive public stock market when the time comes to raise substantial funding for the business.

Without an early-stage stock market, the risk for the venture-capital investor increases very significantly. If an investor knows that a new and exciting company is going to absorb a large investment, say $50 million to $100 million, before it becomes profitable, he will rarely invest. The financial exposure is too great, over too long a period, for the risk involved.

The financial exposure and the risk are both significantly reduced, however, if you know that, as you achieve certain milestones – say, the desired technological breakthrough – then, even though your company is still losing money, you can take it public by selling shares on the stock market. That way, you benefit from the increase in the value of the company to raise additional finance at a lower cost. The venture capitalist's challenge is no longer that of funding the company all the way through to profitability, it has become instead the lesser challenge of funding the company as far as flotation.

The main stock markets cannot deal with high-growth companies that have not yet achieved profits. It is not their business. They exist to trade stocks in large, established companies. The more frequent problems of younger companies are a nuisance to the image of stability that the main stock markets want to project, especially in an economic downturn.

The creation of Nasdaq in 1970 provided a market for young, high-growth companies in the United States and it transformed the risk profile of early-stage investment with spectacular results. In the last forty years, five new, entrepreneurial, hi-tech businesses that floated on Nasdaq have made it to the top 100 companies in the world as measured by market capitalization: Microsoft, Sun Microsystems, Intel, Cisco and Oracle.

Whereas Nasdaq's rules from inception protected the investor against fraud, but left the issue of business risk to the investor, the London Stock Exchange, through its listing rules, has required a track record of profitability in order to protect the investor against business risk as well. This difference of approach made it very difficult for young companies to access the stock market in Britain.

As I have described, the Unlisted Securities Market was established in 1980 to fulfil this role in Britain, only to be closed down by the

London Stock Exchange in 1992. The USM's successor, AIM, is now the only market left in Europe playing the early-stage role.

Its counterparts in Germany (the Neuer Markt) and France (Euronext) both failed, as did Easdaq, with which I was associated. AIM, however, has a number of shortcomings and is still not regarded by some as a serious market. By the end of 2005, Apax had backed only two companies that floated on AIM. By contrast, we had floated thirty companies on Nasdaq, fifteen on the London Stock Exchange, six on the Paris Bourse, five on the Frankfurt exchange, four on Easdaq and two on the New York Stock Exchange.

The reasons for Europe's junior stock market failures are a matter for debate. What is indisputable is that, if you look at the last thirty years, years marked by massive commercial and entrepreneurial advances, Europe has failed to rise to the early-stage and hi-tech challenge.

The only European hi-tech companies to appear in the top 100 companies of the world, as measured by market capitalization, are Nokia, which is an unusual example of an established European company that transformed itself from lo-tech to hi-tech, and Vodafone, which, having been a successful start-up, grew after being absorbed by Racal, which was already a large British public company.

Europe's relative failure in this area, in my view, is to an important degree the result of the absence of a viable European stock market focused on early-stage companies. Despite the efforts of venture-capital firms operating across Europe like Apax, which has now abandoned early-stage investment, and 3i, the sector as a whole is still significantly short of capital compared with the United States.

Some say this is a chicken-and-egg problem, because it is unclear which should come first: sufficient numbers of exciting European

"THIS PLAN ONLY WORKS
IF YOU AGREE TO HELP US
FLOAT, RISE AND GET OUT
AT THE TOP."

This cartoon was featured in Apax's 1994 Christmas card and reflected our frustration at the difficulty of floating high-growth, early-stage companies in Europe. Helped by the creation of Easdaq, Euronext and the Neuer Markt, the hi-tech wave carried us to 52 flotations over the next six years, half in Europe and half in the USA. Easdaq and Neuer Markt have since disappeared.

hi-tech entrepreneurs or an appropriate stock exchange. To me it is obvious that wherever it is asked which came first, the chicken or the egg, the answer is that neither came first: both came at the same time. They are interdependent.

Although private equity in Europe has grown dramatically in recent years (from $8 billion of funds raised in 1996 to more than $100 billion in 2006), the bulk of its investment activity is in mature businesses. In 2005, European private-equity investment in early-stage opportunities was reportedly less than half the amount invested in the United States – $11 billion compared with $26 billion.

In 2006, the figures were better, around $20 billion compared with $31 billion, although the European figure was significantly boosted by the weak American dollar relative to the euro.

For European hi-tech to thrive, we need European venture capital to thrive. If European venture capital is to thrive, we need a European stock market geared to high-growth companies, capable of funding them before they have reached profitability. Such a market needs to have a separate identity and a separate governance structure from the main stock exchanges, even if it is affiliated with one or more exchanges.

Nor can it be designed as merely a 'stepping stone' market that is unsuitable for high-growth companies once they have become successful. The credibility of Nasdaq has been boosted by the fact that Microsoft and others have chosen to stay on it, thereby providing powerful role models for new, ambitious ventures.

The next bounce of the ball for stock exchanges is global con-solidation, going beyond the transatlantic tie-up between Euronext and the New York Stock Exchange. A key question for European entrepreneurs and policy-makers is how to take advantage of this next bounce so as to ensure that the resulting exchanges properly

The chicken and the egg came at the same time

address the needs of European early-stage, high-growth companies, in the way Nasdaq does for their American counterparts.

At what point do you exit? It depends if you are an entrepreneur or an investor. At Apax, I was both. In the early years, our philosophy as investors was to ride the winners for as long as possible. We held one early-stage investment, Computacenter, for thirteen years and made a £250 million gain from it. There are several that we held for ten years or more, including Healthcare At Home. Then, as our investors required us to show a track record whenever we went to raise new funds, the pressure led us to prove our success by selling out earlier.

By and large, that meant investing in more buy-outs, the gain on which could be realized in three to five years. Early-stage investments generally take seven to ten years to come to fruition. Buy-outs, which are mostly large, established businesses, could be transformed by our investment and sold sooner. The buy-out effect that results from the management team being more motivated, more focused on the bottom-line and freer to act than it was within a larger group, can already be significant over two to three years.

From the late 1990s, I had my own exit in mind. Succession presents a separate challenge from that of building up a successful business. I had decided when I was in my early fifties to leave the firm on my sixtieth birthday. The question was how best to prepare my departure so that the firm would continue to thrive.

In the 1970s we had separated the British, American and French offices to enable each of the partners to flourish in his own way.

Twenty years later we made moves in the other direction: back towards a unitary firm. In 1999 we merged all our European businesses except France. In 2004 we merged the non-French European operations with the United States. We reached the stage where we could describe our firm as a leading global player.

There was never a resting place in view; there was always a higher level of success that attracted me. My objective evolved: 'I am not in the early-stage business, I am in the private-equity business; I am not in the UK private-equity business, I am in the global private-equity business' and so on.

I believe in being number one. Getting to be number one was an exciting challenge for me and then for my successors. When I left the firm I said to my colleagues: 'You have the baton now and you have to win the race. You have got to become the recognized leader, the largest and best-performing private-equity business.'

Over the years, individual deals had not always turned out as we expected. But as a whole, with some adjustments in strategy, overshooting at times when markets were hot and undershooting when markets were cold, things turned out as expected. Broadly, did we expect to get the returns that we achieved? Did we expect to build the firm we built? The answer to both questions is yes. Broadly, it worked in line with my expectations, which were always high.

To have achieved an average rate of return for the funds for which I was responsible – after the deduction of Apax's fees and carried interest – of more than 30 per cent a year over fifteen years was an outstanding performance by any measure.

I was not obliged to leave Apax at sixty. The house rule we instituted is that you can stay until sixty unless a fund is being raised while you are still in employment, in which case you can stay for eighteen months after the fund is raised and collect a share of the financial benefits. We were raising a $5 billion global fund when I left. I could have stayed until I was sixty-one and collected a great deal more money. But I felt I ought to stick with the principle of

"WE'RE VENTURE CAPITALISTS FROM A FARAWAY GALAXY...
WE HEARD THE MARKET IS PRETTY HOT ON
YOUR PLANET RIGHT NOW!"

*Our Christmas 1999 cartoon: the hi-tech bubble was about to burst
and our friends from far away had arrived too late.*

sixty. If you want to create a great institution, you stick with your principles.

Hanging on into one's sixties or even later is seldom a good idea. First, from the perspective of the firm, if you have got great people, you have got to give them a timely chance to run the business. If they are ten years younger than you are – if they are forty-five and you are fifty-five – and they know that at the age of fifty they will be able to run the business, you will continue to keep and attract great people and move forward fast. That is what the business requires. Look at Goldman Sachs: people leave now at fifty, to make way for the new generation. At McKinsey they leave at between fifty-five and sixty. There is a rule in professional businesses that if you want to keep your people, and keep on attracting excellent recruits, you have got to give them a decent chance of reaching the top.

Over and above leaving at sixty, I never thought that my epitaph should read: 'He was a great venture capitalist' or, 'He achieved an IRR of more than 30 per cent.' I think I have more important things to do. I want to make a difference in other areas.

Of course, any business imposes its own requirements regarding succession. It was not feasible for me to leave before I was sixty because I needed to merge different entities, recruit key people to replace retirees, organize the election of my successor, and overlap with him for a period while he took the reins and raised our next $5 billion fund. But I was determined not to go on beyond sixty and I prepared for that over several years.

This raises the question: at what point does an entrepreneur admit that it is time to let go?

It is not an academic question. If you do not lead in this, sometimes your team lets you know, and sometimes it is self-evident: decisions are not made, they are not made quickly enough, the decisions made are the wrong decisions, people leave, recruitment gets more difficult. If he does not lead the process, the entrepreneur may misjudge all these signs, but the signs are all there to see.

If you are wholly ego-driven, you will find it hard to acknowledge that you have reached this stage, but if you are focused on the success of the business you will not. I think good entrepreneurs are self-critical. The great entrepreneurs can see that things can be done even better; they have an accurate assessment of their own contribution.

Complicating matters is that significant amounts of money are often at stake and you can find yourself on a fast upward-moving financial escalator, with a high price attached to getting off.

I avoided those kinds of issues. For me, getting out of Apax had to be connected with chronology, not prospective achievement, or I would have stayed forever – the private-equity industry continues to expand and there is certainly a huge amount for Apax to achieve. So I stuck with the deadline of my sixtieth birthday.

Large corporations deal with succession every few years. They know how to do it. But few entrepreneurial firms get it right. Too often, entrepreneurial firms are identified with the founder and cannot survive without him or her.

The basic observation I can make is that succession is a process not an event. Unfortunately, it is most often viewed as an event: that it happens all in one go, on an exact date. If it is to be well handled, it has to be a staged process. Somebody has to be appointed and groomed to take on the leadership role. There has to be a transition of the key levers of the business. Eventually, there is an announcement and, later, a departure date. It sounds easy. In practice, it requires discipline and self-control on the part of the entrepreneur, because succession begins the day it is announced, not on the day it is supposed to come into effect. If your successor is worth his salt, he or she will do as much as possible as quickly as possible during the transition period, and you have to fight the instinct to interfere.

When a founder leaves, he or she should be replaced by someone as good or better, and the firm should go as quickly as possible to the next level. I wanted to leave the firm with a sense of purpose and with people at the helm who were hungry to achieve great things. Matters were arranged so that I left Apax after my successors raised a huge new fund that took the firm another step forward.

There was a first generation of partners at Apax who were getting to retirement age at much the same time as I was. Some left before me, some left shortly after. So we needed to work out a generational succession. It was not only about me. We looked at the composition of the executive committee and we looked at the heads of the industry sector teams, in information technology, healthcare, media and so on, and made succession plans for all of them. We also planned the transition of the membership and leadership of the investment committee, the operating committee and exit committee. We identified the next generation of leaders.

How your successor is chosen is important. Apax has the culture of a partnership: the partners had to decide. The question is, what does it take for the person appointed to have real authority? There are many people in the firm with ambition: the person at the head must command their respect.

I had long ago come to the conclusion that we needed a constitution for the firm. One was agreed in 1998. We decided that the leader should be elected by secret ballot. Candidates would be invited to come forward and would each have the opportunity to make a presentation about the future of the firm. In the event, everyone decided that there was one outstanding candidate for the job, Martin Halusa. I was of the same opinion. Martin made a detailed presentation to the partners about his views and plans and was elected unanimously.

The rule we instituted at Apax is that the leader should be elected every three years. If he stands more than once, the first time he must get 51 per cent of the votes, the second time 66 per cent and the third time 75 per cent. The constitution ensures that succession is a process, one that the firm anticipates. Only in this way can the firm ensure that the strongest people stay knowing that their chance to run it will come.

For fourteen months, Martin Halusa and I worked side by side. It was Martin and the team, not me, who raised the 2005 $5.5 billion fund. It got him off to a good start.

When you run in parallel, if the successor is any good he will take over. As soon as Martin had been announced as my successor and CEO of our European operations, all the power moved to him, even though there was a lengthy overlap period during which I acted as non-executive chairman. Everyone's future then depended on him, not on me. Martin quickly took over responsibilities from me and began to run the business. For me and for the rest of Apax, this was confirmation that he was the right person to lead the firm.

Since leaving, I have not given my Apax colleagues advice unless they have asked for it. My successors have to play their hand the way they want to play it. If the succession has been well handled, there will be powerful entrepreneurial voices at the helm; they will only be asking for my advice occasionally and they will do well. In raising the $14 billion fund in 2007, they took Apax's total funds under management to $35 billion.

When you quit, do you just walk away and shut the door or do you try to manage your departure more gracefully? I kept an office in the Apax building in Portland Place for a year after I left, then moved to a new office suitable for my new career.

Generally speaking, the ability of the entrepreneur improves as his or her business develops. By the time you make your exit, you might be at the top of your game. What do you do next? Do you sit on the beach or do you plunge into another venture, using the expertise and financial resources that your career has brought?

The truth is that, as I observed in the opening chapter, entrepreneurs come in all shapes and sizes. Some entrepreneurs are really capable of doing only one thing well. They may not be particularly good at business outside their own sphere. In that case, leaving the business they built can be difficult. Those who are strongly business-oriented or management-oriented can become serial entrepreneurs. Building businesses is what they do.

Either way, it is hard to keep a good entrepreneur down. Entrepreneurial drive is a powerful force. Entrepreneurs, especially if they have already been successful, are often attracted to the upside inherent in uncertain situations. It is in their blood. Many today are choosing to put something back into society by becoming social entrepreneurs. This is what I had been planning for my life after Apax. I took the first steps in 2000, when I accepted an invitation from the British Treasury to chair Britain's Social Investment Task Force.

Since the end of 2005, I have also chaired the independent Commission on Unclaimed Assets, which includes people from the voluntary and private sectors, and the banks. Our principal recommendation is that we should use the deposits in bank and building society accounts in Britain which have been unclaimed for fifteen years or more in order to create a new institution. This would be an effective investment-banking operation geared to acting as a wholesaler of capital for the social sector. It would drive the development of organizations achieving a social purpose, from philanthropic ventures to those that have a commercial business model serving a social objective.

The idea that this unclaimed money might be used to set up a risk-taking institution, a social investment bank, to support social entrepreneurs is novel. It arises from blending my experience as an entrepreneur with that of other members of the Commission from the voluntary sector, banking and public services.

If you take the basic circumstances that surround poverty in Britain today, and you consider the changing role of government and the private sector, it is perfectly clear that a shrinking state sector requires an increasing social sector, sometimes called the third sector, to deal with social issues. But you cannot attract capital to the social sector in the way that you can to the private sector, because financial return is not the only driver of capital flows. The government has therefore to introduce tax and other incentives. If you are going to have such incentives, it is crucial that there should exist an organization that can apply the incentives to financial products, in order to attract private-sector capital to the financial intermediaries that fund voluntary organizations. A 'wholesaler' of capital for the sector, so to speak, is essential if voluntary organizations are to have a more powerful impact.

Such an institution could, for example, refinance credit unions' loan portfolios. You could take a loan portfolio and give them 80 per cent of the money – because, say, they have a 20 per cent loss rate – and, as a bank, you could sell on that risk to the financial markets as a bond. You could do the same thing with, say, the Prince's Trust: they have, say, an £80 million loan portfolio, they are constrained by their ability to raise money and they have a 40 per cent loss rate. So you could guarantee part of the portfolio and sell it all on to another bank. The Prince's Trust would thus have recycled its capital to fund its operations and to assemble a new loan portfolio. This is an entrepreneurial way of thinking.

Most people in the state sector are inhibited by uncertainty. But if you know you can overcome hurdles – because you have done it before – then you might agree that the situation provides the opportunity for a risk-taking institution of this kind. If you are an entrepreneur, be it in the private or the social sector, you say: 'That is the thing to go for. Let's do it.'

Seen in this way, as I said at the beginning, entrepreneurship is a way of thinking that can be applied to all kinds of avenues in life.

As a result of the work of the Social Investment Task Force, now in its eighth year, I have come to feel that we can only help poverty in deprived areas of Britain if we can attract private investment. In business terms, these poor areas suffer from under-investment. Old industries, whether they be shipbuilding, coal mining, docks or fishing, have died out. There is little if any capital now attracted to the areas that have fallen into decline. The money has stopped flowing but the people have been left behind.

Philanthropy and government incentives can help alleviate their suffering, but philanthropy can only go so far, and government intervention tends to create dependency not independence. The most compelling way to effect economic improvement in the long term is to create businesses that pull people out of poverty, and empower them to take leadership in their communities and to take responsibility for their own lives. They then act as powerful role models for others. Sociological studies have suggested that if positive role models fall below a certain proportion – 5 per cent is the oft-quoted figure – of a specific community, that community spirals sharply into decline. Conversely, anything that creates sufficient positive role models helps to pull communities out of disadvantage.

The level of motivation in these communities is extremely high, higher than in the mainstream economy. What private equity has helped to do in better-off areas it is capable of doing in poorer areas too. As a young social entrepreneur involved in micro-finance, Faisel Rahman of Fair Finance in the East End of London, put it to me, 'People do not want charity, they want a chance.'

With these thoughts in mind, Apax co-founded Bridges Ventures in 2002 with Michele Giddens, who worked with me on the Social Investment Task Force, private-equity firm 3i, and Tom Singh, a successful entrepreneur who built up New Look into a major retail chain. Shortly afterwards, Philip Newborough, who had previously worked at Apax, joined as the CEO. I have chaired Bridges Ventures, pro bono, since its inception. It invests in the poorest areas of Britain, as measured by the government's index of multiple deprivation. In 2002, we raised £40 million, half of it from the private sector, mainly from banks, including HSBC, Citigroup and Lloyds TSB, and pension funds that had backed me in the early days of Apax – the West Midlands Pension Fund and the South Yorkshire Pension Fund – as well as successful venture-capital firms such as Doughty Hanson and entrepreneurs such as Mike Lynch of Autonomy. The family foundation that my wife and I set up invested £1 million. The Department of Trade and Industry matched the private-sector investment with £20 million of government money, almost half of which has a capped rate of return. So far, we have made equity investments in twenty-five businesses employing seven hundred people, of whom two hundred came out of unemployment.

Bridges Ventures is social investment run on commercial lines. As part of the work of the Social Investment Task Force in 2000, I looked at community-development investment initiatives in the United States. The general approach I found there was to aim for blended social and financial returns that you could not really isolate. I saw that these efforts often fell between the financial and the social stools, achieving neither objective in the eyes of the investors who backed them. I thought that this approach would not raise substantial capital in Britain or anywhere else in the long run. In my view, the only way to raise substantial capital was to go to the financial marketplace, targeting a specific financial return while at the same time targeting a social purpose. We could say, 'We will give you a 10 per cent to 15 per cent return, net of fees and carry, so that you will make money but it might be less than you would make by investing in private equity elsewhere. If you combine that return with a properly measured social return, would you be prepared to invest?' The locomotive is the financial return; the carriages are the social return.

The British government sweetened the offer by agreeing that a proportion of the government money should be first in and last out, and in the form of long-term debt. There is no secret about the fact that the purpose of the government money was to reduce the risk for the investor and to improve the return. Without it the private investment would not have been forthcoming. My hope and expectation is that Bridges Ventures will do more than achieve its targeted rate of return. If the management team can get a better return, it is because entrepreneurs in poorer areas have done well and substantial capital will flow into future funds and enable us to make a real impact on poverty. The government should achieve a significantly higher return on its total investment than it receives on long-term government bonds, hopefully encouraging it to repeat the experiment now with half a dozen Bridges Ventures lookalikes.

We are already seeing results. We have had three successful exits:

from the buy-out of Harlands, a failing label-printing business in Hull that had been purchased by its management, whom we backed to turn it round; from the buy-out of a vehicle parts company, H.S. Atec; and from the sale of Simply Switch, a cost-comparison start-up in Croydon.

Simply Switch was founded by Karen Darby, a single mother of three who left school at sixteen with no educational qualifications. With her business partner, Alistair Tillen, and an investment in two rounds of about £300,000 from Bridges, she built a multi-million-pound firm from scratch employing more than seventy people of diverse ethnic backgrounds in a poor part of London. As well as building a successful business and providing employment, Simply Switch has raised more than £500,000 for charities in Britain through affinity partnerships. The business was sold to the Daily Mail and General Trust for £22 million, split more or less equally between Karen, her co-founder and Bridges Ventures.

On the strength of this performance, and after much hard work, we have been oversubscribed in raising a second Bridges Ventures fund, this time without government support. We have again attracted forward-thinking banks, pension funds, hedge-fund managers, venture capitalists, successful entrepreneurs and personal foundations, who between them have put up £75 million.

Bridges Ventures is a new type of investment vehicle that uses a private-sector approach to reduce poverty. The power of these vehicles is this: what drives their social mission is the need to achieve a sufficient financial return in order to attract significant investment to the poor areas they target. I believe that community venture-capital, or social venture-capital as it is perhaps better called, will become an increasingly important segment of the private-equity industry, attracting mission-driven, talented professionals who believe that entrepreneurship knows no social or geographical boundaries, and that if entrepreneurial society is to operate fairly, equal opportunity to be successful must be offered across poor as well as affluent areas, countries and cultures. Without this, a yawning gulf will come to divide rich from poor and the resulting social tension will eventually push governments back to the old and inefficient model of high taxation, low growth and extensive efforts to redistribute income and wealth rather than to create it.

In 2003, I co-founded The Portland Trust, a not-for-profit British foundation, with Sir Harry Solomon of Hillsdown Holdings. The famed historian, Sir Martin Gilbert, joined us soon afterwards as the third trustee. David Freud, who was vice-chairman of UBS Investment Banking, is the fourth trustee and the current CEO. The Portland Trust stemmed from my desire, which I have always considered to be something of a vocation, to address the Palestine-Israel issue. I was born in Egypt. I got thrown out of Egypt as a penniless refugee. I am Jewish, my wife is Israeli, I have deep ties to Israel. It is important to me that Israel thrives and it is important to me that Palestinians should also thrive, that they should have normal lives and not have to put up with the inhumanity that results from the conflict's violence.

Harry Solomon and I decided to create a foundation that would help develop and support economic initiatives to improve the standard of living of Palestinians and poor Israelis, and thereby give the general population on both sides a significant stake in peace. It focuses on the use of economics in peace-making.

The standard of living in the West Bank and the Gaza Strip has remained poor for fifty years, desperately poor. If we can help develop the Palestinian private sector and give ordinary Palestinians, in particular, a better life for them and their families, political

271

moderation will follow. The economics will influence the politics. If there are powerful economic motives for maintaining peace, then the moderates will constrain the extremists. But if there are no powerful economic motives, the extremists will continue successfully to position themselves as the defenders of the community. That is one of the key lessons from the conflict in Northern Ireland, and how that conflict has been moved away from violence towards political discourse. Economics made peace possible there.

In May 2007, the Portland Trust published a study called *Economics in Peace-making: Lessons from Northern Ireland.* We have applied those lessons to Palestine. We have undertaken an analysis of the Palestinian economy that concludes that it is capable of providing jobs and a decent standard of living for all its citizens. Palestinians are an intelligent, well-educated, highly literate people. They have a sophisticated business class and banking system. They have a private sector with real potential for growth. We need to support the Palestinian private sector more than the state sector. Extremists on both sides are happy to attract money into the Palestinian state sector, because it encourages dependency and political patronage. When you interview people in the private sector, they generally want an end to the strife. We have set about working with leading Palestinians to define measures that will help the Palestinian private sector to thrive.

Working with the former Finance Minister and now Prime Minister of the Fatah administration, Dr Salam Fayyad, we set about instituting a loan-guarantee scheme that would absorb up to 70 per cent of any loss on a loan when a local bank lends between $5,000 and $500,000 to a Palestinian business. The scheme provides a $200 million package of guarantees – $29 million from the European Investment Bank and the German KfW, $50 million from the Palestinian Investment Fund and $110 million from American government agency OPIC – that will allow nearly $300 million of loan finance to flow to small and medium-sized Palestinian businesses. The Palestinian economy has a GNP of about $3.8 billion, so the loan-guarantee scheme could have a significant impact on financing its expansion.

We are also supporting the efforts of Dr Salam Fayyad to reform the pension fund system, creating a private-sector pension scheme that will bring the added benefit of accumulating capital for investment.

Another project we are working on is the registration of land and property rights. You cannot get mortgages until you have sorted out the question of property rights. Individual Palestinians ask: 'I have been living here for fifty years, can I please borrow against my property?' But the banks say: 'Where is the piece of paper that says you own your home?' Only 18 per cent of land and property in Palestine is properly registered. We are working to resolve this.

We are also helping to provide microfinance to relieve poverty in Palestine as well as in the north of Israel.

I think The Portland Trust is among the pioneers of an approach that says you can use private-sector techniques to achieve objectives that governments find difficult, because opposing parties are locked in a painful political stalemate.

Just as we in the private-equity industry have climbed a mountain with regard to European attitudes towards entrepreneurship over the last thirty years, I think we as social entrepreneurs can climb a mountain in terms of the perceived risks and challenges of social investment. By bringing in private-sector norms of management and efficiency, we can attract private-sector levels of management talent into the voluntary sector and, with the help of appropriate tax incentives, we can attract significant investment through the capital markets.

I am not saying we can solve all the problems of society in this way, but I am saying that, by backing social entrepreneurs, we can have the same sort of impact on social issues that private equity has had on the mainstream economy.

These examples illustrate a range of social concerns and commitments that I believe are going to become more important in the future. The vast commitment of resources made by Bill and Melinda Gates and Warren Buffett to medical research; the contribution successful entrepreneurs such as Sir Richard Branson, Sir Tom Hunter and Jeff Skoll of eBay fame, who supported Al Gore in producing *An Inconvenient Truth*, are making to public debate; the efforts Bridges Ventures and The Portland Trust are making to alleviate hardship and resolve conflict: all these are part of an increasing range of social-enterprise ventures being driven by entrepreneurs to address issues that hitherto have been viewed as the province of government. I believe that private enterprise will find a new area of opportunity in social investment and I believe that great companies are going to be judged on their engagement with social initiatives. The judges are going to be their own customers, employees and shareholders.

Social investment is going to be a new asset class. I am sure of it. Ten years from now, people will be saying that pension funds, insurance companies and corporations must allocate a certain percentage of their assets to organizations that provide a social as well as a financial return.

I can see that asset class; I can touch it; I know it is going to be there. It is inevitable. Unless the private sector and the voluntary sector can remedy poverty, the system will blow up. Why are prominent entrepreneurs and others picking up issues that governments used to address and applying private-sector business practices to them? Why does Bill Gates decide to leave his business at the age of fifty to devote the next ten years of his life to solving health and social problems? Because he has the confidence he can do it. He built one of the top five companies in the world before the age of fifty. Having done that, he believes that he can apply his entrepreneurial mind to solving problems such as AIDS. Why is Warren Buffett backing him? Buffett knows that it is not the money that counts. Governments have plenty of money. What counts is the entrepreneurial mindset and skill. We are at a sea-change where social investment is concerned.

I have written here about social enterprise, as if it is only entrepreneurs who have an obligation towards society. But, in truth, obligation is not a one-way street: politicians and the major financial institutions have a responsibility also to support and foster enterprise, not just for the sake of the entrepreneurs but for the sake of society as a whole. Enterprise is a huge social force. As I think I have demonstrated in this book, its impact can be transformative, for nations and communities as well as for individuals. Within the right legal framework, it can also be a powerful lever for democracy, as is being demonstrated today in the former communist-bloc countries.

It is a case of 'two cheers for capitalism'. Capitalism may not be the most perfect system for society, but it is the best system anyone has come up with. In the United States there is no ambivalence about this. By contrast, every European country to a degree is still schizophrenic in its attitude towards capitalism and wealth creation. Many Europeans hanker for some other, perfect system that will deliver equal benefits for everyone. Meanwhile, the reality is that much of Europe is driven by the economic and technological dynamism of the United States.

I am now sixty-two and I have the freedom to use my resources and my entrepreneurial ability to help deal with social issues that matter to me. I am one of a swelling number. In fact, more or less the whole generation of entrepreneurs who prospered over the last thirty years are now turning their attention to social investment. We are the early build-up of a major new wave.

In building the private-equity industry, we had to work with government and regulators to create institutions and initiatives that would work in our favour. The British Venture Capital Association, a new British structure for onshore pension funds, options legislation to encourage entrepreneurship, venture capital trusts, Tony Blair's involvement in encouraging institutions to invest in early-stage ventures, Gordon Brown's reduction of capital gains tax and his calling for the implementation of the Myners Report (which recommended that institutions should invest in private-equity funds), lobbying for the formation of appropriate stock markets: there is a whole series of initiatives that we have undertaken, encouraged or supported in the course of our professional lives to amplify the entrepreneurial wave. Those skills are now applicable to this new wave of social entrepreneurship.

There are few entrepreneurs who cash in and retire to a beach house. It is in the nature of the entrepreneur to do rather than to be.

You will find that, having made a successful exit from your business, you will channel your energies in different directions. You will lead an active life. You will continue to thrive on high adrenalin and high levels of activity. In fact, the fate of most entrepreneurs is to be busier after they have sold their business than they were before. Previously they had confined their activities to one venture, now they are pushing in several different areas.

At the beginning of this book, I promised that I would lay down the 'higher-level rules, the fundamentals of entrepreneurial strategy'. You might ask, how come I have hardly mentioned strategy at all? How is it that I have not passed on the secrets of market positioning, price points, financial leverage, product differentiation and so on? Are they not the essence of entrepreneurship?

Frankly, no. Target markets, price points, debt ratios, product differentiation: these are tactical issues.

The specific strategy for your particular business depends on the nature of your business. The fundamentals of strategy that are applicable to all entrepreneurial businesses are to be found on the preceding pages. If you look back over these ten chapters, you will find that business strategy is at the heart of all my observations. First, have an accurate assessment of your own inclinations and abilities. Are you a person who prefers to climb the North Face or do you prefer the easy route? If you prefer the easy route, entrepreneurship is not for you. Do you regard risk as uncertainty that provides opportunity for greater profit or do you regard it as a four-letter word that has the connotation of running into danger? If fear of failure seriously inhibits you, entrepreneurship is not for you.

If you are equipped to be an entrepreneur, calibrate the opportunity and pick your timing. Go for the largest opportunity in the largest market. Recruit the best team in your industry. Do not be afraid to recruit people who are better than you at their jobs. Draft a rugged business plan that can cope with unexpected problems and test it hard. Do the necessary due diligence and then do some more. Get an accurate measure of the length of financial runway you will need to take off. At stage one, raise enough money to get you to stage three. At stage two, raise enough money to get to stage four. Raise the money from the most experienced, most reputable source you can find. Begin to plan your exit even as you make your entrance. Listen to your intellect and intuition and control your ego. Make it your business to be a good student of your sector and of the economy as a whole. Make your own luck by persevering, building a network, learning from your business, being adaptable, staying focused, and most of all by turning every setback to your advantage. Adhere to the highest ethical standards and create a sense of obligation in your team to do the same. Make an orderly exit, like a relay runner passing the baton to his team-mate as he accelerates away, giving him the best chance to win the race. Above all, anticipate the next bounce.

There, in a single paragraph, is how to turn risk into opportunity.

Like a runner
who passes
the baton cleanly,
give your
successor
the best chance
to win

Index

Compiled by Sir Martin Gilbert

Apax, 99, 109–11, 224; and the British
market, 225
Giddens, Michele: 268
Gilbert, Sir Martin: 271
Gladwell, Malcolm: 195
global economy: 15–16, 221–2, 256,
258
global funds: 2, 96, 215
Goldman Sachs: 24, 261
Google: 41, 70, 73–4, 75, 192
Gore, Al: 274
Gosford Park (film): 85
government bonds: 3
Greece: 186
'greed, hypocrisy and moral laxity':
236
Grosvenor House Hotel (London): 26

HSBC (Hongkong and Shanghai
Banking Corporation): 268
H.S. Atec (vehicle parts): 270
Haji-Ioannou, Sir Stelios: 66, 129
Hale, Dr Hamish: 135
Halusa, Martin: 139, 263
Harel, Sharon (Sharon Harel-Cohen):
85, 271
Harel, Yossi: 112
Harlands: 270
Harpo Inc.: 292
Harvard Business School (HBS): 13, 14,
15, 18, 52, 87, 89
Harvard Law School: 16
'haves and have-nots': 241
Healthcare At Home: 33, 35, 258
hedge funds: 99, 100–1, 102, 221
Henry Fellowship: 13
Hewlett-Packard: 78, 238
Hicks Muse: 185
Hill Samuel: 26

Hillsdown Foods: 71, Hillsdown
Holdings: 205, 271
hi-tech: industries, 14–15, 16, 192–3, 254;
bubble, 29, 31, 111, 118, 143, 260; and
venture capital, 30, 31, 252, 256; and
hope, 104; cartoon, 260
Hollywood: 236
home market: 224–7
Hong Kong: 105
Hoover: 60
Hull: 226, 270
human genome: 31
Hulme, Phil: 126, 127
Hunter, Sir Tom: 274
Hutchinson: 105
hybrid engines: 99

IBM (International Business Machines):
40, 77–8, 97, 103, 180, 208–9, 219, 222,
223
ICI (Imperial Chemical Industries): 40,
134
IPO (Initial Public Offering): 56, 91, 98,
109, 127, 186, 250–1
IRR (internal rate of return): 181, 261
ideas: and execution, 171
incentives: 139
income tax: 19, 28, 35, 36, 37, 42
'indecent haste': 118–9
India: 82, 96, 217
information technology (IT): 14, 46,
97–8
Inmarsat: 39, 186
innovation: 30
Institut de Dévelopement Industriel
(IDI): 18–19
institutional investors: 100
integrity: 248
Intel: 15, 41, 103, 253